JOY TO THE WORLD

GOD'S GLOBAL MISSION
FOR LOCAL CHRISTIANS

PHILIP M. BICKEL

CONCORDIA
PUBLISHING HOUSE

Copyright © 1989 Concordia Publishing House
3558 S. Jefferson Avenue, St. Louis, MO 63118-3968
Manufactured in the United States of America

Library of Congress Cataloging in Publication Data.
Bickel, Philip M., 1948—
    Joy to the World: God's global mission for local Christians, Philip M. Bickel.
       p.   cm.
    Bibliography: p.
    ISBN 0-570-04534-7
    1. Missions. I. Title.
BV2061.B53 1989
266—dc20

2   3   4   5   6   7   8   9   10   98 97 96 95 94 93 92 91 90

Contents

Preface

If you could write a book on any topic of your choice, what would you write about? Had you asked me that question two years ago, I would have replied, "I would love to write something that would motivate fellow Lutherans to love the world as Christ does."

I remember the day in 1979 that God gave me a heart for the world. For ten years I had had a strong interest in evangelism, but only recently had I begun to catch glimpses of the global dimensions of the Gospel I believed and shared. The turning point came when I saw statistics which revealed that the church is a long way from making disciples of all nations. Until then I had thought that we were only involved in mop-up operations. So much more needed to be done, and God was willing to include me in His world mission adventure. Since then my family and I have experienced a variety of mission activities: refugee settlement, lifestyle evangelism in Mexico, a missionary assignment in Venezuela, and today perhaps the most difficult mission task of all—lifting the gaze of a typical, middle-class congregation to see the cross-cultural opportunities both close at hand and at the ends of the earth.

At times these assignments have brought headaches, fatigue, and discouragement, but through it all there has been an underlying current of joy. The joy of knowing that we are exactly where God wants us to be; the joy of shining our light in a dark place; the joy of knowing that the perishing are discovering Christ's salvation as the Holy Spirit illuminates their hearts and minds to believe.

You hold in your hand the fulfillment of my desire to write about God's mission. Surely, the Lord has kept His promise: "Delight yourself in the Lord and he will give you the desires of your heart" (Ps. 37:4). My continued desire and prayer is that through these pages our Lord would involve you in Christ's global adventure and grant you His mission joy.

In the service of the King of kings,
Philip M. Bickel
All Saints' Day, 1988

Acknowledgements

I express deep appreciation to all who contributed to this work. First place goes to my wife Julie and our three children, Katy, Sam, and Kristy. Thank you, dear ones, for sharing the cross-cultural experiences the Lord has given us and for caring about those who are perishing without Christ.

Second place goes to my fellow missionaries and my brothers and sisters in the Lutheran Church of Venezuela. I praise God for the privilege of having served Christ with them. A special thank-you is extended to Missionary Dana Brones, whose real-life globetrotting adventure inspired chapter 2.

I owe a debt of gratitude to Pastor Ron Rall, whose recommendations to Concordia Publishing House resulted in the opportunity to write this book.

Special recognition goes to the two dozen people who read the initial manuscript and offered helpful criticisms. Whether lay people, clergy, or missionaries, all provided me with helpful perspectives from which to view the text.

Insightful stories and observations were provided by LCMS missionaries through information shared with me directly or through the Board for Mission Services. In particular, I offer grateful thanks to Rosemary Althoff, Roger Buck, Steve Burke, Walt DeMoss, Dennis Denow, Becky Hsiao, Doug Johnstone, and Todd Roeske.

This book was the major project in my studies toward the Doctor of Missiology degree at Trinity Evangelical Divinity School, Deerfield, Ill. Many thanks to the professors at Trinity for their contributions to this text. Gratitude is also expressed to Aid Association for Lutherans for their generous full-tuition scholarship.

Grateful acknowledgement is made for use of the material from the following:

Key to the Missionary Problem by Andrew Murray, © 1979 Leona F. Choy (Ft. Washington, PA: Christian Literature Crusade). Used by permission.

Communicating Christ Cross-Culturally by David J. Hesselgrave. Copyright © 1978 by David J. Hesselgrave. Used by permission of Zondervan Publishing House.

Chapter 1

The Joy of Salvation

The Greatest Missionary Ever

The missionary candidate surveyed the view from the highrise office window of the mission headquarters. Far below, the multitudes wandered like sheep without a shepherd.

Stepping up behind the candidate, the executive director of the mission rested a hand on his shoulder and reflected, "To be sure, you will be leaving a lot behind so that you can bring them the Good News. You will forsake the comforts of home and set aside the honor and prestige that you have here. And many of them will wish you had never come. It won't be safe."

"I know," replied the candidate, "but when I think of those who will be saved through my efforts, I feel a great joy. All the suffering will be worth it."

"I'm glad you feel that way," said the director, moving to his desk. "However, there is one more detail about your assignment which we need to discuss. It is rather unusual, but I trust you will be willing. Please have a seat."

The candidate took a chair quietly and waited for the director to continue.

"Allow me to remind you that a missionary must strive to identify with his people and with their culture to such an extent that he becomes one of them. That is the goal, even though up to now it has been impossible to attain it perfectly."

"Yes, sir," agreed the candidate, "but tell me about the unusual part."

"Here it is. There is one way to close the gap completely between us and them, a way to become thoroughly joined to the people and their culture." As the mission director continued, his voice swelled with the conviction and enthusiasm of a decision-maker with a bold new strategy.

"What we need is a volunteer willing to enter your mission field in a unique manner—as an infant. He will have to forsake all his adult capabilities and be born among them, weak and helpless. In this way, he will learn the language and the culture from the very first step. Of course, this will mean years of waiting before you can preach the Word and sacrifice yourself, but when the time finally comes, you will be one of them. . . . Yes, I know it is quite unusual, but it will work! Well, what do you say, my son? I have a body prepared for you."

"Here I am! I have come to do your will."

The two beamed at each other. Then, turning to his intercom, the director ordered, "Angela, get me Gabriel on the line. I have some messages for him to deliver."

Although the decision to send the Son of God to earth did not actually occur in this fashion, this hypothetical conversation underlines one key fact. Our Savior, Jesus Christ, was a missionary. If God were not a missionary God, there would have been no incarnation. Heb. 3:1 advises us, "Fix your thoughts on Jesus, the apostle and high priest whom we confess." What does the word *apostle* mean? One who is sent. What does *missionary* mean? One who is sent. So even the Scriptures give Jesus the title of missionary (Kane 1986, 78, 84). Christ surely deserves the title of the Greatest Missionary Ever.

No missionary ever left more behind than He did. No one ever had to cross a wider cultural chasm. None of us ever had to suffer as He did. Without this missionary we would all still stand condemned before God. None of us would have been saved if this cross-cultural worker had not crossed the chasm between the worlds in order to die on the cross in our place. Thus He earned the right to charge us with the task of going to all the nations to make them His disciples.

Why was Jesus willing to endure all the culture shock and all the opposition? Heb. 12:2 tells us that Jesus took all the risks, including the shame of the cross, "for the joy set before him." What joy? The apostle Paul defines a missionary's joy: "For what is our hope, our joy, or the crown in which we will glory in the presence of our Lord Jesus when he comes? Is it not you? Indeed, you are our glory and joy" (1 Thess. 2:19–20). Paul is saying that his joy is people who have come to be saved through the preaching of God's word. The joy set before Jesus was the same—*people,* the people for whom He gave His lifeblood: you, me, and people from every tribe, tongue, ethnic group, and nation.

An Invitation to Joy

Christ, the greatest missionary ever, rejoices in us. With our salvation assured, we gladly join in singing mission hymns, such as

> Joy to the world, the Lord is come!
> Let earth receive its King;
> Let ev'ry heart prepare him room
> And heav'n and nature sing.

How many Christmas seasons have you sung this hymn with gusto, rejoicing in the good news that Christ the Savior is born? But "Joy to the World" is not only a Christmas carol. Its global perspective qualifies it to be a mission hymn every bit as much as "From Greenland's Icy Mountains." The joy of salvation by grace through faith, not works, is intended for all the inhabitants of this planet we call home.

8

If our Savior God were only a local tribal deity with limited geographic influence, we would have to sing

> Joy to my town, the Lord is come!
> Let my corner of the world receive its King;
> Let ev'ry one from my culture prepare him room
> And the United States and Canada sing.

This was never God's plan, however. "The earth is the Lord's, and everything in it, the world, and all who live in it" (Ps. 24:1). "And we have seen and testify that the Father has sent his Son to be the Savior of the world" (1 John 4:14). Our God loves the world. Christ is a world Savior. The Holy Spirit was sent to make us witnesses to the ends of the earth. Since the triune God is a world God, we ought to be world Christians.

This book is an invitation to live as a world Christian. And what is that? A world Christian is a believer who, laying aside all provincialism, recognizes the global nature of God's Law and Gospel. The world Christian prays, "Lord, You sent Christ to be the atoning sacrifice for my sins, and not only for mine but also for the sins of the whole world (1 John 2:1–2). Therefore use me to see that Your saving word gets out to everyone on this earth."

Some readers might jump to the conclusion that I am out to recruit missionaries, but that is not the case. A missionary is a Christian who crosses barriers of language and culture in order to share the love of Christ. A world Christian may or may not be a cross-cultural missionary. In fact, the vast majority of world Christians are not missionaries. Most of them remain at home while eagerly supporting cross-cultural missionaries through their prayers, gifts, friendship, and concern.

God does not call all His children to be missionaries, but He does expect them all to be world Christians. Perhaps you have heard it said that Christians cannot choose whether or not to be witnesses for Christ, because they are so automatically. The issue is, Will their words and actions give a positive witness or a negative one? Being a world Christian is similar. All Christians are automatically world Christians. The question is, Will we be faithful ones or not? Some believers have not fully accepted their role as world Christians, because of ignorance, fear, or unwillingness. Maybe the task of reaching the world for Christ seems just too gigantic to them. Perhaps they do not know how or where to start. For some, apathy has more appeal than sympathy for the lost. The following chapters aim to rectify many of these problems.

The purpose of the present chapter is to assure you that being a world Christian is the highest joy anyone can experience this side of Christ's return. This is not an overstatement. Consider what the Bible teaches about joy.

Jesus the Joyous

David exults, "You turned my wailing into dancing; you removed my sackcloth and clothed me with joy" (Ps. 30:11). The King James Version uses the word "mourning" instead of "wailing." Both terms describe the agonizing sorrow of death. Our world is a world in mourning, because people constantly are dying.

In materialistic North America, unbelievers try to hide from the inevitability of death as long as they can. Their blind faith in possessions is proclaimed on bumper stickers: "Life is a beach!" "The one who dies with the most toys wins!" But man does not live by bread alone. Nor do we live by cars, condominiums, and credit cards alone. Other people, who sense the emptiness of materialism but have not yet filled it with Christ, label their bumpers with this dreary conclusion: "Life is a bitch and then you die." As fatalistic as this philosophy is, it approaches the Biblical statement that death is "the shroud that enfolds all people, the sheet that covers all nations" (Is. 25:7).

However, the global plan of our Almighty Creator is to remove that shroud and turn earth's mourning into dancing. In His grace, He sent Jesus the joyous, whose arrival brought joy to the world. The angel announced to the shepherds, "I bring you good news of great joy that will be for all people. Today in the town of David a Savior has been born to you; he is Christ the Lord" (Luke 2:10–11). The wise men from the East experienced the same jubilation. "When they saw the star, they were overjoyed. On coming to the house, they saw the child with his mother Mary, and they bowed down and worshiped him" (Matt. 2:10–11).

In Nazareth, near the beginning of His ministry, Jesus read a prophecy regarding Himself. It stated that He was come to bestow "the oil of gladness instead of mourning" (Is. 61:3). Day after day, for three years, He proved the truth of those words by bringing joy to multitudes.

Then Jesus the joyous came to Gethsemane, where He declared, "My soul is overwhelmed with sorrow to the point of death" (Matt. 26:38). With just cause His soul was overwhelmed, "for the wages of sin is death" (Rom. 6:23), and He was about to pay that wage for all humanity on the cross of Golgotha. This agony He endured in order to "destroy him who holds the power of death—that is, the devil—and free those who all their lives were held in slavery by their fear of death" (Heb. 2:14–15).

When He rose from the dead, joy reigned! The women "hurried away from the tomb, afraid yet filled with joy, and ran to tell his disciples" (Matt. 28:8). That night, when He appeared to them behind closed doors, "they still did not believe it because of joy and amazement" (Luke 24:41), but finally the truth sank in and the joy persisted. And why not? Christ's victory over sin and death fulfilled Isaiah's prophecy of everlasting joy:

> On this mountain he will destroy the shroud that enfolds all peoples, the sheet that covers all nations; he will swallow up death forever. . . . In that day they will say, "Surely this is our God; we trusted in him and he saved us. This is the Lord, we trusted in him; let us rejoice and be glad in his salvation" (Is. 25:7–9).

All praise to Jesus the joyous, our risen Savior! Mourning has been turned into dancing for all who repent and trust in Him. He has removed our sackcloth and clothed us with joy.

Called to Multiply the Joy

Yet that is not the end of the story. Jesus left His disciples with the marvelous duty of sharing and multiplying His joy:

> All authority in heaven and on earth has been given to me. Therefore go and make disciples of all nations, baptizing them in the name of the Father and of the Son and of the Holy Spirit, and teaching them to obey everything I have commanded you. And surely I am with you always, to the very end of the age (Matt. 28:18–20).

This Great Commission is a command to spread the joy from person to person and from nation to nation so that every child and adult on earth has the opportunity to hear the life-giving word of God.

The book of Acts reports that as the early Christians obeyed Christ's command, the joy of salvation was multiplied. The three thousand converted on Pentecost "broke bread in their homes and ate together with glad and sincere hearts" (Acts 2:46). When Philip the Evangelist preached in Samaria for the first time, "there was great joy in that city" (Acts 8:8). Shortly afterward, Philip shared the good news about Jesus with an Ethiopian official. The Holy Spirit called the African by the gospel, and following his baptism, he "went on his way rejoicing" (Acts 8:39). On Paul's first missionary journey, the truth of Christ was proclaimed in Antioch of Pisidia, and the new "disciples were filled with joy and with the Holy Spirit" (Acts 13:52). On his second journey, Paul and Silas declared to the suicidal jailer at Philippi, "Believe in the Lord Jesus, and you will be saved—you and your household" (Acts 16:31). The result? The jailer "was filled with joy because he had come to believe in God—he and his whole family" (Acts 16:34).

Down through the centuries and around the globe, the infectious joy of salvation has spread from heart to heart, and it is still being shared today.

A North American Lutheran of Lithuanian heritage devoted over three decades of his life and $60,000 to translate and publish the Bible in contemporary Lithuanian. His efforts were fueled by joy.

In Marxist Ethiopia the Christian church is growing phenomenally in the midst of severe governmental pressure. Mekane Yesus Lutheran Church of Ethiopia has expanded from 100,000 adult members to 500,000 in only a few years. With joy, many in that land of drought are drawing water from the wells of salvation (Is. 12:3).

Pastor Salimo Hachibamba is the principal of the Lutheran Bible Institute and Seminary in Zambia, Africa. He has a special place in his heart for this school, for it is his alma mater. In 1965 he arrived at the school as a young man, with no financial resources, clamoring for an opportunity to receive further education. Religion had not played a major role in his decision to attend there; but as Salimo studied, the Word of God worked faith in him, and he was surprised by Christ's joy.

Hundreds of civilians fleeing the battle zones in El Salvador find refuge in a haven operated by Resurrection Lutheran Church. There they see Christian love at work and learn about their Savior, *El Salvador*. Peace with God, which many of them now enjoy, will aid them in rebuilding their society when peace returns to their land.

South Koreans exercise their joy at 4:00 a.m. when they rise in throngs to praise their God and plead for His Spirit to open the hearts of unbelievers both in their land and beyond. With such dedication, it is no wonder that South Korea has one of the fastest growing Christian populations in the world.

A husband and wife in rural Minnesota make a point of inviting foreign exchange students to their home. The hosts always have a gift for the students: an explanation of the Christian faith accompanied by a Bible in their native language. Recently, an exchange teacher taught in their area for a semester. Sung was an English instructor from the People's Republic of China. Upon receiving a Chinese Bible from this couple, Sung literally jumped for joy, for he had long desired to investigate this book.

Yes, to know Jesus Christ is to know the joy of salvation. To share Christ with others, whether near or far, is to multiply that joy. And when we are involved in multiplying it to others, our own joy overflows. This is the incomparable joy of being a world Christian. Even though Martin Luther never heard the term *world Christian,* he aptly defines its meaning:

> When a Christian begins to know Christ as His Lord and Savior, . . . then his heart is permeated with God, so that he is driven to help others receive the same, because there is no greater joy for him than this treasure that he now knows Jesus.
>
> So he heads out in every direction, teaches and urges all others, boasts about the Gospel, and witnesses of it to everyone, pleads and sighs that they might receive such grace.
>
> He . . . contests for and strives with all his might, as one who lives for one purpose, that is, that he might spread more widely among people God's honor and praise (Korinth 1980, 367, translation by Ottomar E. Bickel).

Brother Martin contends that the joy of knowing Christ is an emotion that sets us in motion to share Him with others.

Unfortunately, many Christians experience this joy only on occasion. A sermon or book on witnessing motivates us temporarily to be more caring and outspoken Christians. A mission festival at our church inspires us for a time to pray for the salvation of people who are different from us. Our mission joy shines more intensely for a season, but then the flame dies down and only the pilot light is left burning.

Jesus said, "You are the light of the world" (Matt. 5:14). May the following pages stoke the fire of your mission joy, so that it may shine constantly even to the darkest and most distant corners of the earth.

Do Something Now

Telling is not teaching. Listening is not learning. It is in doing that we grasp hold of truth. Therefore, each chapter of this book will end with a series of suggestions for action learning. Some of them take only a moment. Some are more time consuming. From the smorgasbord of activities choose the ones that appeal to you. For further information about the resources mentioned, consult the list at the end of this book.

1. *Search Scripture.* Read Isaiah 12 thoughtfully. In verses 1–3, circle the words which speak of God's grace or the joy of being saved. In verses 4–6, circle the words which speak of proclaiming that joy. Share your findings with someone else.

2. *Read. On Our Way Rejoicing* by Ingrid Trobisch relates the adventures of a large Lutheran family who dedicated their lives to proclaiming Jesus Christ around the world. Though they faced many trials, their joy was always multiplied. Consider how such joy might illuminate your life and that of your family.

3. *Listen.* Try singing a familiar song with a little twist to it. First sing "Jesus loves me." Then sing it "Jesus loves them." What difference does the change make?

4. *Look.* Order for personal viewing or for use in your congregation the film *Salifu's Harvest,* produced by The Lutheran Church—Missouri Synod (LCMS). In this film you will witness the joy of over one hundred people in Ghana, West Africa, as they are baptized into the Christian faith.

5. *Converse.* In conversations with other Christians discuss mission awareness events such as mission festivals, fairs, and conferences. Ask them about the emotions they feel when they are reminded of the need to reach out to those who are lost in sin and unbelief. How long do the emotions last? What makes them go away? What makes them last?

6. *Pray.* When you thank God for saving you, include the concept of joy in your praises. When you pray for the conveying of His good news to the whole world, include the concept of joy in your petitions.

Chapter 2
A World in Need of Joy

When Christians hear *missions,* they are faced with a mammoth challenge. Scan the following verses and you will see the challenge, especially in the italicized words:

> Declare his glory among the nations, his marvelous deeds among *all* peoples (Ps. 96:3).

> And this gospel of the kingdom will be preached in the *whole* world as a testimony to *all* nations (Matt. 24:14).

If God expected us to announce the good news in many countries, that would be a grand enough assignment. But—imagine!—His intention is that every tribe, tongue, people, and nation should hear. What a relentless God we have! He wants all men, women, and children "to be saved and to come to a knowledge of the truth" (1 Tim. 2:4). That was His plan when Paul penned those words to Timothy, and God has never changed His mind.

How are we going to respond to this challenge? Being scientific North Americans, we reach for our pocket calculators and try to grasp the matter mathematically. If we do so, we may reach two mistaken conclusions.

Calculation No. 1: Tapping the calculator keys, you may compute: "There are about 215 nations in the world. And there are Christians found in 195 of them. That means we have completed 90 percent of the job."

Conclusion: "There is no reason for me to be very concerned about missions, because all that is left is mop-up operations."

Result: Nothing is done.

Calculation No. 2: "There are 5.2 billion people in the world." Tap, tap, tap. "Nuts, that number doesn't even fit on this little calculator. I'll use a pencil instead. . . . Okay, 5,200,000,000. There are roughly 1.6 billion people who claim to be Christians. Oh my, that leaves 3.6 billion that face eternity without Christ's cleansing pardon."

Conclusion: "We have been working at this thing nearly two thousand years, and we still have reached only 30 percent of the world. What's the use! The world is so big and the goal so unattainable. Why break your heart in a hopeless cause?"

Result: Nothing is done.

Even though the above calculations are mathematically accurate, both conclusions are false, and the results are disastrous. Yet many Christians have made these mistakes. They leave a mission festival or lay aside a magazine

14

article on missions, concluding that the challenge is either too small to bother with or too gigantic to tackle.

How can you gain a proper understanding of Christ's global mission challenge to His church? Statistics can be useful, and we shall consider many figures throughout this book. But let us above all look at people: the people who live and breathe with us under the same sun, the people for whom God's Son gave His precious blood.

In order to catch the vision of Christ's global mission challenge, we would benefit from eyeball-to-eyeball contact with real people around the world. Of course, few of us have the opportunity to be globetrotters. Therefore, I invite you to learn about the world through the fictional account of one young man.

Al, a Young Man on an Adventure

Al grew up in a Christian home, attending a Lutheran church in Minnesota. Confirmed at fourteen, he was a robust, energetic teenager who liked to dream. And what a dream Al had! He and a friend named Jack wanted to travel around the world, just for fun and adventure. They had talked about it for several years, and when high school graduation arrived, in spite of their mothers' objections, they stuffed their backpacks and booked passage to Australia.

The first three months down under were rocky. Away from home for the first time, Al and Jack found their independence hard to control. Although they did not fall into any grave sins, they spent far too many hours in Australian bars and squandered their money. When their assets dipped to the danger point, they awoke to the fact that they were not accomplishing what they had planned. This excursion was to be the experience of a lifetime, and they had been wasting it.

Wanting to start fresh in a different culture, they took a ship to New Zealand and hitchhiked all over this land of green, rolling hills and snow-capped mountains, meeting many wonderful people in the process. Al and Jack could have stayed there forever, but their hearts and imaginations were drawn by the prospect of the many more peoples and cultures that lay before them. So they landed construction jobs and saved up in order to finance the rest of their journey.

Just when they were about to strike out across the world, bad news arrived from home. Jack's father had had a heart attack, and Jack was needed at home to help run the family business.

What was Al to do? The logical thing, the cautious thing to do was to hop on the same plane with his buddy and head back home. But being on the threshold of fulfilling his dreams, Al was not about to be cautious. Spreading out his map, he reasoned, "I've gone halfway around the world, but all I've seen is water and two English-speaking countries. Ahead are Indonesia, Indochina, India, the Middle East, Europe—all the places I've wanted to see,

15

to hear, even to taste and smell. If I go back the way I came, I'll miss all the adventures that await me. Even though I'll be alone, I've got to forge ahead!''

So Al struck out on his own with youthful zest. Though some people would consider this a foolhardy decision, the Lord watched over His child and brought him safely through all his travels. But most important, during the next twelve months the Holy Spirit gave Al something that he did not expect, something that every Christian needs—a heart for the world.

Come along with Al and learn what he learned.

Papua New Guinea

En route from Australia to Papua New Guinea, Al daydreamed about what he would see there: Stone Age people in loin cloths, witch doctors, maybe even cannibals—from a safe distance, of course. Walking the streets of Port Moresby, he was a bit disappointed. Most of the people wore Western garb, and there was hardly a thatched roof to be seen. However, the biggest surprise was the large number of churches in Port Moresby. When Al spotted a chapel of the Gutnius Lutheran Church, he felt compelled to enter, hoping to find someone who might explain the strange things he had found in Papua New Guinea.

Fortunately, Akii, a church member who spoke English, was present and welcomed the young traveler. After getting acquainted, Al ventured to ask, "Why are there so many churches here, Akii? I thought New Guinea was a heathen land.''

"*Heathen* would have described us even forty years ago,'' Akii replied, "but the gospel of Christ has set us free from the dark ways we inherited from our ancestors. We are now a Christian nation, blessed with faithful missionaries and our own pastors.''

"I had no idea,'' Al responded. "But up in the mountains and back in the jungles there must still be headhunters and cannibals, right?''

"Yes, there are still some unreached tribes, but 90 percent of us belong to some Christian church. In fact, one in six Papuans is Lutheran, like you and me. It is true that some are tempted to go back to the old practices of Satan, and others are tempted to abandon the Savior for the new allurements of Satan being imported from the Western nations. We need good Biblical instruction and counsel to help immature Christians avoid these traps. But, all in all, it still can be said that Papua New Guinea is one of the most Christianized nations in the world. Praise God for that!''

That evening Al returned for a youth gathering at the church. The devotion and faith of the young people were clearly evident. There was no denying that Akii had told him the truth. At the close of the meeting, Al spoke up, "Thanks for letting me see the Papuan church in action. It's nice to know that missionaries have met with success. The job of telling the world about Christ must be almost completed, right?''

"You shall see for yourself as you travel from land to land," Akii responded. "How I would love to go with you. You have a unique opportunity, Al. You have learned something about the people of God in my country. Why not make a point of trying to learn a little about the Christian church in each of the lands you visit?"

"I'd never thought of that before, Akii. When I planned this trip, all I intended to see was new landscapes and exotic peoples, but I'll try to do what you suggest. Thanks for the advice."

Indonesia and the Island of Bali

Heading west from Papua New Guinea, Al began to explore the islands of Indonesia, the fifth most populous nation in the world, with 168 million people. Indonesia, although located five thousand miles east of Mecca, has more Muslims than any other country in the world. In fact, Indonesia is about 80 percent Muslim.

Al traveled mostly by train or bus. The vehicles would be stuffed with people of poverty, along with their chickens, goats, and bags of grain. Some trains poked along at a tedious pace, and others had many holes in the floor, not just the one used for the commode. Often the trains were so crowded that Al would travel for hours without sitting down, and sometimes he would sleep in the luggage racks. He looked at old and wrinkled men and women who had endured this treatment all their lives. For these people it was a way of life—for him it was torture. However, once he accepted the torture as the price necessary for learning about the people, his willpower and patience were renewed. If he had not made this decision, he never could have endured the thousands of miles of bus and train rides that awaited him (Brones 1973, 4).

Although he rarely met people who spoke English, he eventually learned that God was doing marvelous things in Indonesia. In 1965, there had been a Communist coup, followed by a bloody Muslim reprisal. Meanwhile, the few Christians had been peacemakers. This event had led many nominal Muslims to turn from their traditional beliefs. As a result, the Holy Spirit has converted more Muslims in Indonesia than anywhere else in the world. Indeed, nearly 10 percent of the people are now Protestant.

This good news buoyed Al's spirits. He learned that there are even three million Indonesian Lutherans, the result of German missions. Thus far Al was ready to conclude, as many do, that the church had done its duty and the goal of the Great Commission was almost fulfilled.

Then he journeyed to Bali, an island in which 90 percent of the 2.5 million inhabitants are Hindus. Al's arrival was opportune. He was just in time to witness a high religious festival, a blend of Hinduism, Buddhism, and animism, in which the Balinese people worship and appease hundreds of deities. Artistically the festival was a delight, with sacred dances, statues constructed with foods, and giant mosaics of rice-dough cookies; but spiritually, the festival was a dark charade of occult practices and demonic bondage. On the last great day of the festival, two dozen priests offered prayers and sacrificed scores of animals, including an eagle and an anteater, to appease Rudra, a demonic manifestation of the island's supreme being (Miller 1980, 419). Unnerved by the whole experience, Al hoped that Bali was only a rare exception to the progress being made by Christianity.

Calcutta and Nepal

For Al and his conclusion about the near fulfillment of the Great Commission, India was like a kick in the teeth.

The first shock was Calcutta and its ten millions. The city evidenced poverty and squalor at every turn, bearing witness to its namesake, Kali, the Hindu goddess of destruction. Most heart-wrenching was the sight of the one million who live their entire lives on the sidewalks. They are born there, grow up, have children, and die right there. When the drenching monsoons fell, throngs fled to the train depots to protect themselves from the powerful rain. When the downpours lasted all night, the people literally slept on top of one another. For Al the pictures on the cover of *Time* and *Life* magazines had become real; they would no longer be forgotten by turning to the sports or entertainment sections (Brones 1973, 5).

It was not only the wretched poverty that disturbed our young traveler. West Bengal, the state of which Calcutta is the capital, is the home of nearly sixty million people, and only slightly more than 0.1 percent are Protestant Christians.

The day he spent at the Ganges River was an experience never to be erased from his memory: funeral processions arriving to cremate the dead and spread the ashes on the sacred river; people bathing in the polluted waters to obtain spiritual cleansing; people reverently bowing to the sacred cows that meandered everywhere. The spiritual darkness was oppressive. It occurred to Al that this tragic scene had been reenacted every day for thousands of years. In spite of the heat, he shivered at the thought.

If the island of Bali was a puddle of paganism, Calcutta and West Bengal seemed like a sea. But the ocean of need called *India* awaited him. One of every seven people in the world is Indian—750,000,000 people crammed into 2.4 percent of the world's land mass. By the turn of the century, the home of the Taj Mahal and the Himalayas will house more people than China. And religions? Hindu, 82 percent; Muslim, 12 percent; Christian, only 2.6 percent (Johnstone 1986, 215-16).

Al had learned a bit about Hinduism from high school friends who dabbled in meditation and the Hare Krishna cult. His buddies had raved about Hinduism as a high and mystic philosophy. But they did not realize that only the high castes know this kind of Hinduism. Across India Al witnessed the religion of the masses: idolatry on an enormous scale with 33,000,000 different deities venerated and multitudes of sacrifices and rites for purification. But, Al inwardly grieved, no one was ever thereby cleansed of sin. A Bible verse learned years before came to mind: "We have been made holy through the sacrifice of the body of Jesus Christ once for all" (Heb. 10:10).

Al's sightseeing could not be complete without his heading north into Nepal to see Mount Everest. His dreams of climbing the lower slopes of that great peak were dashed by an attack of malaria. With shivering tremors racking his body, he entered a missionary hospital in Katmandu, the capital of Nepal. As he spent four days receiving a sequence of shots and quinine tablets, he thought of all the people who did not even know what a hospital was or who could not afford the fee which to him was only a day's wage. Finally, the treatment was sufficiently effective for him to continue traveling, though in a weakened state (Brones 1973, 6).

Lessons in New Delhi

After leaving Nepal, Al journeyed to New Delhi. On Saturday he searched for a Christian church and worshipped there on Sunday morning. After the Bible study, a hospitable and well-educated elder named Vinoba invited him to dinner, a kindness which Al gratefully accepted. Following the delicious meal of curried rice, Al ventured to ask the questions that were fomenting inside him.

"With millions of Hindus and Muslims on all sides, why hasn't the church in India grown larger?"

"It has grown in some places," Vinoba answered. "In the southern state of Kerala 20 percent are Christian, including churches that were apparently founded by the apostle Thomas. The most Christianized states are in the far west of India; Manipur is 30 percent Christian, and Nagaland, amazingly, 80 percent."

Al was somewhat impressed by this news, of which he had been unaware. But he was not satisfied. "Why then haven't those Christians evangelized the rest of the country?"

"Why haven't the Christians of other lands done so?" Vinoba countered.

"Maybe because we aren't Indian. It would be much easier for you and the believers of Kerala, Manipur, and Nagaland to reach India."

"How do you know it would be easier for us?"

Flustered, Al struggled to control his frustration. "You are all Indians, aren't you? You all share the same country, customs, and languages."

Vinoba chuckled. "My son, you have all the idealistic impatience that comes from being both young and an American. You have been gazing at India these last few weeks, but let me tell you the truth that lies underneath your limited impressions. India is not one culture; we are many peoples all living under the same roof. The masses of India speak 18 languages in 700 dialects. Furthermore, the caste system has us segregated into islands of humanity that do not touch each other. Do you understand, my son?"

"I'm trying to. Do you mean that for Indian Christians to reach other Indians with the gospel, they need to cross wide cultural barriers too?"

"Yes."

"Hmmm. . ." Al fell into deep thought and then recalled, "On the wall of my church back home we have a map of the world, and all the countries where my denomination is working are colored blue. I had always assumed that meant the whole nation had been reached."

"The map misled you, didn't it?" Vinoba offered perceptively.

"I always figured that once a number of churches had been established in part of a nation, those Christians could eventually reach the whole country. Since Christianity is established in at least a corner of almost two hundred nations, I thought the job was almost finished. Perhaps everybody back at Zion Lutheran thought that way."

"We once had a map like that, Al, but we tore it down when we realized that Christ did not send us to countries but to peoples."

"What's the difference?"

Vinoba reached for the teapot. "Have another cup, my friend, and I will explain. The Lord Jesus told us, 'Go and make disciples of all nations.' Do you know which Greek word He used when He said 'nations'? "

"Can't say that I do, Vinoba," Al shrugged.

"The word is *ethne*. What English word does that sound like to you?"

"*Ethne, ethne,* . . . ethnic?"

"Correct. The word *ethne* leads us to recognize our responsibility to proclaim the good news of Christ to all the world's different ethnic peoples: groups who share a common language, culture, philosophy, and world view. The apostle John emphasizes ethnicity in Rev. 7:9 when he says, 'There before me was a great multitude that no one could count, from every nation, tribe, people and language, standing before the throne and in front of the Lamb.' "

"I see. The targets should be ethnic peoples, not simply the political nations that belong to the United Nations. But how many ethnic groups are there?"

"Good question. The anthropologists tend to divide peoples in different ways. But the U.S. Center for World Mission has determined that there are 24,000 different cultural units in the world. Here is a riddle for you, my young friend. In how many of those people groups is there a community of believers with sufficient size, resources, spiritual maturity, and evangelistic zeal to proclaim the gospel to everyone in their culture?

"I have no idea, Vinoba. Before I left home, I would have guessed over half. But now, who knows?"

"Those who care know. Let me tell you, for I believe that you care also. Of the 24,000 ethnic groups, only about 8,000 have a strong Christian community. That leaves 16,000 nations to go. They are the unreached peoples of the earth, living and dying with little or no opportunity to hear the precious name of Jesus proclaimed in a manner they can understand. In India there are 3,000 major people groups, and the Christian church is still weak or nonexistent in over 2,900" (Johnstone 1986, 218).

The numbers struck Al like a bolt of lightning. It seemed as though scales of blindness were falling from the eyes of his heart, as they had for the apostle

Paul after his conversion on the road to Damascus. With a flash of amazed comprehension, Al knew he would never be the same again.

"Let me explain it in another way," Vinoba continued, "so you can understand more fully. There are 5.2 billion people in the world. How many claim to be Christian?"

"I think it's about one and a half billion."

"Very good, 1.6 billion to be exact. Now there is a myth I have read in some Christian books. It is said that if every Christian were to bear witness to Christ and lead one other person to trust in Him, then there would be about three billion believers. Then if those three billion could each evangelize one more, . . ."

"We would get the job done," Al interrupted. "I've heard that idea from my pastor. It sounds logical to me. So why do you call it a myth?"

"Because it overlooks the cultural, ethnic factor. Listen closely. The 1.6 billion Christians are culturally close to only about one billion other people. I'm talking about the Christians' friends and neighbors who talk and act and think much the same as they do."

"And the other 2.6 billion?"

"They speak different languages from the Christians. They have unique customs, ideas, and religions. It does not matter how far away they live. Though they may be near or far, their culture is different, and they will only be reached by some compassionate disciple of Christ who dares to cross the cultural barrier."

"Missionaries!" Al interjected. "For Indian Christians to reach all their countrymen, they will have to be missionaries every bit as much as the Westerners who came here."

"You have learned well, my son. As you continue on your travels through God's world, may He teach you this truth in your heart as well as in your mind."

From Nightmare to Awakening

As Al hopped on the train headed west, he felt good about the lessons he had learned in New Delhi. Years before, when he and his friend Jack had dreamed about globetrotting, they had imagined many exotic sights and bizarre experiences befalling them. But never had Al dreamed about learning the reality of world missions. He was starting to see the world as God saw it. However, the truth must be learned in the heart as well as in the mind, as Vinoba had intimated.

Still weak from his bout with malaria, Al had decided to travel quickly through India by train and stop only in a few major cities before going on to Europe. For a while, Al chatted with a turbaned Muslim gentleman. "How brave you are to travel alone," the Muslim commented.

But then the elderly fellow dozed off, and Al stared out the window. The train passed through town after town. India is a nation of towns and villages.

21

Seventy-five percent of the populace live in India's 600,000 villages. Vinoba had told him that in northern India there was one church for every 2,000 villages (Johnstone 1986, 218). That tragic statistic depressed him.

"Rat-tata-tata-tata . . ." the wheels clicked along the rails.

Visually, the scenery became monotonous. Spiritually, the scenery became frightening—village after village—hungry child after hungry child—Hindu shrine after Hindu shrine—Muslim minaret after Muslim minaret—pagan home after pagan home—eternally lost multitude after eternally lost multitude. Mile by mile, Al's heart shattered into 750,000,000 pieces.

"If the whole world were only India," he groaned to himself, "the Great Commission would still be overwhelming. Satan holds sway here unchallenged. It's as if Jesus had never died on Calvary for the sins of these people. It's as though He had never risen from the dead, never ascended into heaven, never sent His Spirit to baptize the nations. This land and so many others are famine stricken, having never heard of the Bread of Life who can satisfy the hunger of their famished souls" (Lankenau 1928, 7).

" 'Go and make disciples of all nations.' No way! Christ must have been deluded to think it ever could be possible. Just look at all those people! . . . No, I can't stand to! This knowledge is too awesome, too burdensome, too crushing. I can't look anymore! I *won't* look anymore!"

In desperation Al pressed his eyelids shut with all his might and clamped his hands over his ears to drown out the sound of the foreign tongues being spoken by his fellow passengers. How blessed it felt to escape from India for a moment, to escape from reality! After ten minutes his muscles tired of shutting out the world, so he lowered his hands from his ears, still refusing to look at the Christless Indian villages.

Eventually, he dozed off and dreamed. How vivid it was! His folks were throwing a homecoming party for him. Spellbound, everyone listened to him talk about his travels. His buddy Jack admired, "Al, you sure were courageous to leave me and go see the world alone!" How proud and brave their adulation made him feel!

"Rat-tata-tata-tata. . ."

Regaining consciousness, Al knew he was not home. He also knew that he was not brave.

"You might say I'm gutsy in a cross-cultural sort of way," he mused with his eyes still shut tight. "How else could I be enjoying this trip? But my Christian faith doesn't have a lick of courage to it. Why, I'm not even brave enough to look out the window."

Then the Holy Spirit compelled Al to look. He could not weep with his eyes shut.

"O Christ," he cried, as the Indian scenery blurred with his tears, "the burden is more than I can bear. But it is not more than You can bear. You bore the weight of sin and hell for every one of these people I see. Help me to look, and look, and look again until I can begin to love the world as You love it."

He prayed that petition over and over as the train bustled on past the crowds for whom his Savior had willingly given His lifeblood. Al looked and looked until the truth was branded on his soul: These people were his brothers and sisters, and he and all other Christians had been brought to faith by the Spirit to love and lead these lost ones to the Redeemer.

Finally, the train reached the end of the line. As he put on his backpack, the turbaned Muslim gentleman spoke to him kindly.

"I noticed your tears. Are you homesick?"

"No, sir, but thank you for your concern. I've just been learning that the whole world is my home."

"Ah. That is a good lesson, indeed. Well, good-bye. The blessing of Allah be with you, young man."

"May the blessing of Jesus Christ be with you, sir."

The Near East

Proceeding through Pakistan, Iran, Iraq, Syria, and Turkey, Al discovered more of the Muslim world which he had witnessed earlier in Indonesia. In the early centuries of Christianity, these lands and also all of northern Africa had been filled with thriving Christian churches. However, as time passed, these churches became lethargic and infected with false teachings. When the waves of Muslim conquest began in the seventh century, these churches fell under the menace of the Muslim sword. Only a few withstood the pressure to convert to Islam. Today they total fourteen million Christians, but most parishes are plagued by dead formalism and a survival mentality.

Al personally witnessed the grim truth of these statistics. Minarets and mosques abounded; hardly a church was to be seen. In fact, in all the 4,500 miles from Pakistan to Morocco, there are nearly 275,000,000 Muslims, but perhaps only 10,000 people from a Muslim background have converted to Christianity (Johnstone 1986, 70-71). "Those are mighty slim pickings," Al mused, "when Christ commanded us to bring in a full harvest."

Although the Middle East needed God's Word and Sacraments as much as India, Al was not overwhelmed and frustrated as he had been earlier. The reason was not that he had become callous to the spiritual need. In fact, he was more sensitive than ever to these people who believe in one god, Allah, but reject the saving work of Jesus Christ and the sanctifying power of the Holy Spirit. Having begged God to give him a heart for the world, he was now able to look without wilting before the harsh reality.

Eastern Europe

Al had journeyed the length of Asia, the least Christian of all the continents. Upon reaching Eastern Europe, he expected that now things would be different. After all, Europe is the "Christian continent," isn't it?

Well, things were certainly different. Although still foreign compared to North America, the people, architecture, and language were much more familiar to Al than the many cultures he had experienced in Asia. Just as he had expected, the cities and the country landscapes were dotted with churches. Unfortunately, many of the churches in Bulgaria and Romania had been confiscated by the communist government and were being used as warehouses or museums.

While dining at a small restaurant in Bucharest, Romania, Al had a most enlightening conversation. Having finished a delicious pork stew with corn flour dressing, he was just digging into a generous slice of *brinzoaica* (cheese cake), when a girl about his own age approached him.

"Excuse me, sir, you are a foreigner, are you not?"

"I am an American."

"May I sit down, please?" the girl asked, seating herself without waiting for an answer, and furtively glancing around at the other tables to be sure that no one had taken notice of her action.

"Forgive my poor manners," she apologized with a whisper. "But watching you from a table across the room, I noticed that you prayed at the beginning of the meal. Are you a disciple of the Lord Jesus Christ?"

After a pause Al replied, "Well, I've never said it that way before, but yes, I am."

"Praise God!" the young lady quietly rejoiced. "I am Sofica, also a disciple of the Lord Jesus Christ."

"Hello, my name is Al."

"Al, my brother in the faith, do you have a Bible?"

"I have a small New Testament," Al answered in a normal voice, but Sofica signaled for him to speak softly. Half whispering, Al continued, "It is in English, not Romanian. Why do you need it?"

"Do you not know how rare the Word of God is in Communist lands? Whole shipments of legally imported Bibles have been recycled to make toilet paper (Johnstone 1986, 357). Therefore, even an English Scripture is a treasure. When you travel from my land, you can purchase another New Testament, so would you please, out of love for God, give me yours?"

"You make it sound illegal."

"It is illegal for someone to import Bibles without a license. However, it is not illegal for you to accidentally leave your New Testament somewhere and for a Christian such as me to accidentally find it."

Amused at Sofica's interpretation of the law and touched by her need, Al said, "I will make a deal with you. I will give you my New Testament if you will take a few minutes to tell me about the church in Eastern Europe. Agreed?"

"Agreed, but the conversation must be brief. Anyone speaking to a foreigner is suspect. Throughout Eastern Europe the government bombards people with atheistic propaganda. As a result, the number of Christians has declined. However, there is an increased spirituality and commitment on the part of all those who take the risk of being a believer."

"What kinds of risks?" Al asked.

"Persecution takes many forms: loss of jobs, loss of scholarships, some

Christian parents have their children taken from them, some are exiled or imprisoned, and others are committed to mental hospitals. The government pressure is intense in Romania. Informers infiltrate the churches. Pastors and church leaders are falsely accused of crimes and blackmailed.''

"I know that communists are atheists. But why do they hate Christianity so much?''

"Marx taught that with the advent of communism, religion would wither and die. Communism also teaches that it will bring into being a new man, that is, people who are truly hardworking and concerned about the welfare of others. Unfortunately, they are no closer to the new-man dream now than they were at the time of the Bolshevik Revolution of 1917" (Bockmuehl 1980, 151-52).

"I don't follow," Al interrupted. "What does this new man business have to do with the church?''

"Communism cannot make a new man. Atheism cannot make a new man. Only God the Holy Spirit can do this. While non-Christian workers often have problems with alcoholism and the like, Christians tend to be the most dedicated laborers, who give aid and advice to those workers who are troubled. This is true in Russia, in the Eastern bloc countries, and even, we have heard, in China. Do you see? We who have been saved through the washing of rebirth and renewal by the Holy Spirit are new men and women, and it galls the communist leaders that the power of God is doing what they cannot ever accomplish. That is why they persecute us so much.''

"Now I understand why many people in my country hate the communists,'' observed Al.

"Hate is for the godless. The Holy One who gave His innocent blood for us commanded, 'Love your enemies and pray for those who persecute you' (Matt. 5:44), and Saint Paul said, 'Do not be overcome by evil, but overcome evil with good' (Rom. 12:21). We shall lead our persecutors to God only by demonstrating the love of Christ.''

"You are right. You are right," Al repeated thoughtfully. "Thank you for your observations, Sofica. When I walk out of the restaurant, I shall just happen to leave my New Testament on the shelf where people place their hats. But do you know something, Sofica? You hardly need a Bible, because you already have it memorized in your head.''

"No, my brother, it is not just in my head but also in my heart. Thank you!''

Western Europe

After traversing the beautiful land of Yugoslavia, Al crossed into free Europe. There he noted that the magnificent churches were not used as warehouses. How content he was with this pleasant change—until he attended worship in a large Lutheran church in Germany.

The Gothic structure with its beauty and grace testified to the faith of the earlier generations that had constructed the edifice to the glory of God. But inside there were only 192 people. Al counted each one, because he could not believe it—192 people echoing hymns and prayers through the cavernous emptiness of the chancel.

However, the 192 were not unfriendly. At the conclusion of the worship service, several of them attempted to speak with Al, but his four years of high school German did not help much. Then two of them, Franz and Lydia, tried their high school English on Al; and they spoke it quite well, because after all, English was only one of the four languages which they could speak.

After general conversation, Al inquired, "How many members does this church have?"

"Our parish lists about four thousand on its rolls," Lydia replied.

Sure that he had misunderstood, Al asked her to repeat the figure, but the answer came back the same—four thousand.

"Then why in the world was the attendance so poor?" Al asked.

"Poor!" Franz retorted. "This was a pretty good crowd."

"Where, then, are all the rest?"

Franz and Lydia proceeded to inform Al about the spiritual atmosphere in the state churches of Europe. A living relationship with God through Jesus Christ is something that is rarely taught or sought. Yes, there are some thriving Christian congregations, but they are a minority. Though multitudes are baptized and listed as members, active participation in the life of the congregation is not considered to be important. America has C and E Christians, that is, those who come on Christmas and Easter. In Europe the vast majority are B, C, W, and F Christians: those who assume that they only need to darken the door of the church for baptisms, confirmations, weddings, and funerals.

During the rest of his stay in Europe Al learned more about the spiritual climate of Europe. Both atheism and the occult are gaining strength at the same time, because people who believe in nothing will be taken in by almost anything. In France, for example, there are more spiritistic mediums and fortune-tellers than there are medical doctors. Furthermore, Al was amazed to see a number of mosques, the largest situated just outside of Vatican City. Indeed, Muslim proselytizers are finding Europe a ripe field for expansion. Al had previously imagined that Europe was the Christian continent, but he saw enough to convince him that it was a post-Christian continent. "Europe needs to be re-evangelized," Al concluded. "for many people here are as pagan and as far from the kingdom of God as those I saw in Asia." (Kibira 1984, 21)

A Change of Course

The day finally arrived for Al to head home. Seated in the Paris airport with a ticket for New York in hand, he reminisced about his trek. Regretting that the adventure was about to end, his thoughts were interrupted by an announcement: "Flight 351 leaving from Gate 47. Destination: Lagos, Nigeria, with stopovers at Algiers and Monrovia."

"Flights headed for Africa?" Al questioned, digging out his map that was now as wrinkled as a magazine in a barber shop. Studying the geography, he talked to himself, as people who travel alone tend to do. "I hadn't realized that Africa was so close. Why, Nigeria is roughly half the distance to Minneapolis. It sure would be great to see Africa." The wheels of his mind whirred.

"On the one hand, I'm tired of traveling. I can hardly take in any more sights or experiences. On the other hand, when will I ever be this close again? How can I go around the world and skip the whole continent of Africa? And South America too for that matter," he added, glancing at the land mass to the west of Africa.

He weighed his options while lightly waving the ticket to New York. At that moment a dark-skinned family walked by in the corridor, and Al found himself wondering what their home was like.

"I'll do it!" he cried out so energetically that the woman next to him dropped her 700-page novel. As he strode to the ticket counter, he fleshed out his plan. "I'm too tired to see the whole continent, but a few countries will be better than nothing. Then I'll catch a boat for South America and at least see Brazil."

West Africa

Someone once said, "Africa is a feeling" (Warnke 1966, 184), and Al tried to capture as much of that feeling as he could while traveling through the West African nations of Liberia, Ivory Coast, Ghana, and Togo. He learned that to speak of Africa is to speak in superlatives. It is the continent with the highest birth rate and the highest death rate. There are over 1,700 languages and dialects, 32 percent of the world's total. Africa has enormous problems: faltering agriculture, the encroaching Sahara, and 18 countries whose economies are in a state of collapse (Johnstone 1986, 44).

Al's last stop was Nigeria, the home of one of every six Africans. The city of Lagos amazed him with its five million inhabitants. When Al commented on the city's size to a hotel clerk, the clerk remarked, "Pardon me for saying so, sir, but the urbanization of Africa is a fact of which most foreigners are ignorant. Nigeria has 25 cities of a hundred thousand or more, and Africa is 28 percent urban. By the turn of the century, most of us Africans will no longer live in green jungles but in what you Americans call concrete jungles."

A continent of superlatives. A continent of drastic change. That is Africa. But the greatest change in Africa is rarely mentioned in the world's news media. In one century Africa has become the most Christian continent on earth. In 1900, only 3 percent of Africa was Christian. Today, 40 percent confess Christ. Some experts estimate that the majority of the continent will be Christian by the year 2000.

But all is not rosy in Africa, as Al learned one day from Mr. Ekong, a church elder: "The church has three powerful opponents in Africa. One is Islam, which is sending more and more of its missionaries into sub-Sahara Africa. Another enemy is revolutionary socialism or communism. The weak economies and growing urban problems of Africa make many people ripe for the communist ideology. Indeed, Islam, communism, and Christianity are locked in a three-way battle for the souls of Africa."

"What is the third opponent?" Al questioned. "The third is syncretism. This is a mixing and merging of the truths of the Christian faith with the traditional religious beliefs of the people. Many people have said that they believe in the God of the Bible, but they have not left the old ways. They have not abandoned the idols and spirits of traditional African religions. Their problem is much like that which Israel experienced in the Old Testament. They wanted to worship both Jehovah and the idols such as Baal. In Africa we need many faithful Elijahs to direct people to the true God."

"So, Mr. Ekong, even though Africa has great potential, it also faces great obstacles," Al concluded.

"Precisely! Pray for us, my son."

Brazil

From Lagos Al caught a steamer headed for Sao Paulo, Brazil. Upon arrival, Sao Paulo's sixteen million people overwhelmed Al. The congestion and pollution of the city testified to the fact that it had grown up so rapidly that city planners had had no time to plan sufficiently for the millions who had thronged to this "land of opportunity." A full one-third of the populace lived, or rather barely survived, in the *favelas*, or slums, that surrounded the city.

Remembering that there was a new Lutheran seminary in the city, Al asked directions until he found the *Escola Superior de Teologia* of the Evangelical Lutheran Church of Brazil. On that beautiful campus, he made friends with several students who spoke some English, and between classes they showed him the sights.

The students showed him the *favelas* up close, as they went to preach at churches in the slums. One thing that amazed Al was that in Brazil he felt almost middle-aged, because the population was so young. His friends informed him that this was typical throughout Latin America. The population is booming, because advances in health have reduced infant mortality. However, child care is not advancing accordingly. In the slums Al saw ample evidence that 19 percent of the children in Sao Paulo are either completely abandoned or must fend for themselves most of the day.

One evening at a Brazilian barbecue restaurant Al remarked to his friends, "I had always thought that Latin America was all Catholic, but now I see that there are many Protestants here, including lots of Lutherans."

Al's observation was greeted by a roar of laughter from the students. "What's so funny?" he asked.

Leopoldo, who spoke the best English, explained the reason for their outburst. "Al, you have jumped from one misconception—the idea that all Latin Americans are faithful Catholics—to another wrong conclusion. Let me explain. The main reason that there are almost one million Lutherans in Brazil is that many Europeans came to settle here. Today we are gaining converts from the non-European populace of Brazil through personal evangelism, the media outreach of the Lutheran Hour, and social ministries. This situation does not exist in other Latin American countries. Lutherans there are a small minority. In addition, God has caused the other Protestant churches of Brazil to grow marvelously. Today our country is 17 percent Protestant, a figure that no one would have believed twenty years ago."

"So growth is occurring only in Brazil?" asked Al.

"Not only here. Chile and Guatemala have been blessed even more than we. They are about 20 percent Protestant. But in most other Latin American countries the Protestants are a struggling minority."

"In those other countries, then, the Catholic Church is dominant?"

"Yes and no," Leopoldo replied. "Although most Latin Americans would say that they are Roman Catholics, in many countries the people do not practice their religion. For example, it is said that in Peru only 20 percent are active Catholics, in Bolivia 12 percent, in Uruguay 10 percent, and in Venezuela only 8 percent."

"This is surprising news to me," Al admitted, sipping his drink.

Filipe, another student, spoke up. "Al, what most outsiders do not realize is that neither Catholicism nor Protestantism is the major religion of South America."

"Then what is?"

"Religions such as Umbanda, Macumba and Kardecism."

"What are they?" Al asked, scraping the legs of his chair on the floor as he leaned forward to hear better above the samba music.

"They are the major spiritistic religions of Brazil. When you went through Africa, Al, you must have seen examples of how the people fear spirits and offer sacrifices to them so that no harm will come to them."

"Yes. It was mighty weird stuff," Al affirmed.

"Those very same religions were brought to Latin America by black slaves. The African beliefs were then mixed with similar ideas of the natives here, resulting in religions like Umbanda and Macumba, which emphasize the casting of magic spells and the contacting of spirits in seances. And many of the better educated and affluent are adherents of Kardecism, a European form of spiritism. Here in Brazil, 60 percent of the people practice some form, including many people who claim to be Christian."

"But this is only in Brazil, right?" Al asked hopefully.

The whole group shook their heads in response, and Filipe spoke up, "Similar religions are found throughout Latin America. For instance, I have a friend who is a missionary with the Lutheran Church of Venezuela. He says that in the middle of the major freeway through the modern city of Caracas, there is a statue of a muscular, naked lady riding a wild pig and holding a pelvic bone aloft in her hands. She is Maria Lionza, the major spiritistic goddess in Venezuela. My friend says that 25 percent of the people give their allegiance to her. Twice a year over 50,000 devotees gather on a sacred mountain to worship Maria Lionza with all manner of occult practices."

"It is the same in other countries," Leopoldo added. "The names of the gods and goddesses may change, but the result is the same—millions of people believe a lie of Satan, a lie that costs them the peace with God that they could have through faith in Christ. So, Al, even though the church is growing in Latin America, there is still a lot of work to do."

Coming Home to the World

A week later Al waved good-bye to Leopoldo, Filipe, and his other friends, as he boarded a plane headed home. During the long flights to Miami and then to Minneapolis, Al felt as though he were dreaming two separate dreams at the same time—one of them about a home he could barely recall, and the other about a world he would never forget. He jotted down his thoughts:

Lord, I began this journey on a lark, just for fun and adventure. But you have made it a pilgrimage of faith. I have been exposed to the marvelous wonder and beauty of Your perfect creation: the mountains, the flowers, the forests, and the sea; the people, the laughter, the joy. But I have also seen how man in his sinfulness can ruin it: the filth, the poverty, and the obscenity; the injustice, the crying, the heavy hearts.

I have lived in their homes and have warmed myself by their fires. If only I could go back and give them the remedy for their struggle—the only effective remedy, the Gospel of salvation through Jesus Christ. If only they could hear about a different life, life eternal with You (Brones 1973, 1, 9-10).

Nobody getting off Flight 614 to Minneapolis received a more excited welcome than Al got from his parents and sisters. After praying for him every day for sixteen months, they were thrilled to have him home. Showered with questions about his journeys, Al felt overwhelmed.

"I know you want to talk. And I want to talk, too. But right now too many emotions are flooding over me. If you don't mind, would you just let me be quiet and think until we get home?"

"All right," his mother answered understandingly. "Just as long as your father and I can put an arm around you as we walk to the car, to assure ourselves that you are really back."

"Sure!" He placed one arm around his mother's waist, and another on his dad's shoulder.

As they walked, Al noticed an Hispanic sweeping the floor. At the baggage claim a Vietnamese flight agent checked his claim ticket. Walking out of the terminal, they passed an American Indian family, apparently headed out on a flight. Sixteen months ago, Al might not have noticed these folks, but now they seemed to be shouting for his attention.

During the drive home he reviewed his journey: the rough beginnings in Australia; the hundred and one cultures; the friends he had made, such as Vinoba, who had told him of the world's need for Christ; the train trip from New Delhi that had begun as a nightmare and resulted in his waking to face the challenge of the Great Commission.

Al would have continued his reminiscing, but his eye was attracted by buildings and signs: an Isuzu dealer, a Thai restaurant, a Jewish synagogue, a Korean Tai Kwan Do martial arts school, a Chinese laundry, and the Islamic Center of Minneapolis.

Al's dad pulled into the driveway and shut off the engine. No one spoke for a moment, and then Al prayed out loud, "Thank You, O God, for keeping me safe all the way home, home to this mission field."

"What do you mean, son?" his dad asked.

Al began to explain.

Do Something Now

1. *Search Scripture.* Make a study of the passages where Christ commanded us to go to all the world: Matt. 28:18–20; Mark 16:15–18; Luke 24:46–49; John 20:21; and Acts 1:8. Note the similarities and unique features of each reading.

2. *Read.* You will learn more about unreached peoples, and how the church can reach them in such books as *Take a Giant Step: Be a World Christian.*

3. *Listen* to the cassette "Our Ministry: The Global Mission Challenge" by Dr. Edward Westcott, executive secretary, the Board for Mission Services of the LCMS. Compare the contents of this message with what you learned from Al's story.

4. *Look.* Obtain a world map or a globe and put it on display in a place where it will serve as a continual reminder that God loved the whole world so much that He sent Christ to redeem everyone. Try to get a Peters map or some other map that shows accurate sizes of the continents, rather than those which stretch the Northern Hemisphere out of proportion (e.g., Africa should appear larger than North America).

5. *Converse.* Find people who have traveled to another country and chat with them about their experiences. Endure their slides, if you can. Chat with them about the people of that land and their need to know Christ.

6. *Pray.* To pray more intelligently regarding the global work of the church, obtain the book *Operation World: A Day-to-Day Guide to Praying for the World* by Patrick Johnstone. This book is both a Christian world almanac and a detailed prayer list for the nations. Your prayer life will reach new horizons. (All materials mentioned above appear in the Resource List.)

Chapter 3

Obstacles to Mission Joy

Through Al's experience you have learned how far we Christians are from attaining the goal the risen Savior set for us. We have *not* preached the good news to all creation (Mark 16:15), because 2.6 billion human beings lie outside the influence of our preaching. We have *not* made disciples of all nations (Matt. 28:19), because 16,000 cultural groups have not been sufficiently penetrated by the gospel. Unfortunately, there is a wide gap "between World Evangel-*ism*, which is working away at the job, and World Evangel-*ization*, which is getting the job done. Finished! Period!" (Board for Communication Services 1986, 5).

In response to this news, some readers might object, "You said in Chapter 1 that missions was a joyous topic, that being a world Christian was life's most thrilling activity. But Chapter 2 was one of the most unsettling stories I have ever read. Joy! You have to be kidding. I just feel frustrated, guilty, and burdened."

Frustration, guilt, and a sense of burden have hindered the mission joy of many Christians, leaving them overwhelmed, incapacitated, and discouraged. If you are frustrated, you are not alone. I, too, have been baffled by the immensity of the task. If guilt is gnawing at you, you are not the only one who has felt that way. I wrestled with mission guilt for many years. If you feel burdened, remember that all world Christians bear a burden for the lost, but they have learned how to cope with it.

In this chapter you will learn how the Lord overcomes our frustration, removes our guilt, and helps us bear the burden. As you read, "may the God of hope fill you with all joy and peace as you trust in Him, so that you may overflow with hope by the power of the Holy Spirit" (Rom. 15:13).

The Frustration That Saps Our Energies

Frustration is the anguished feeling of helplessness that Al experienced on the train leaving New Delhi. He longed to escape by closing his eyes to the vast, mind-boggling challenge. This is not unusual. Even the veteran world Christian occasionally feels overwhelmed by the magnitude of the work to be done.

We need to learn how to overcome our frustrations, so that they do not suffocate our desire to see the day when "the earth will be filled with the knowledge of the glory of the Lord, as the waters cover the sea'' (Hab. 2:14). So let's learn how to deal with three common frustrations.

1. I thought we were almost done

This attitude is expressed in the complaint, ''You mean we *aren't* almost finished? I was under the assumption that we had reached almost all the world.''

Some call this assumption ''The Comfortable Doctrine.'' It makes us feel successful and obedient. We assume that if some unbelieving person wants to know about Christ, he needs only to walk a few miles to the local church and inquire. In many parts of the world, this is false, because (1) there is no local church; or (2) the Christians who meet there speak another language, have a different culture, or belong to a different social class than our hypothetical inquirer.

Many lay people and pastors believe the comfortable doctrine, sincerely assuming that it is true. I confess that I myself was guilty of this misconception during my first four years as a pastor. The comfortable doctrine is very popular for three reasons.

First, there is the statistical mirage, mentioned earlier, of thinking only in terms of political entities Christians have entered (195 of 215) and not in terms of ethnic groups with thriving indigenous churches (only 8,000 of 24,000).

Second, in the 1950s and 1960s rising nationalism influenced the course of world evangelization. While colonies clamored for self-rule, in like manner national churches campaigned for independence from missionaries and Western mission boards. Droves of missionaries were called home, and many Christians concluded that the age of missions had ended. In general, independence has benefited the churches overseas. However, instead of sending the missionaries home, the mission boards should have reassigned those who were willing, to new pioneer mission work among unreached peoples.

Third, the comfortable doctrine is just that—*comfortable*. To reach all nations, we would prefer to believe that little or no effort is required on our part. In contrast, the truth that Al learned is quite uncomfortable and calls for personal involvement and sacrifice.

> A *world* Christian isn't smarter or better than other Christians. By God's grace he has made a discovery so unsettling and unacceptable to him as a disciple who loves his Lord, that he will never be the same. He has discovered the great gulf between what our Lord asked us to do for Him and what we are getting done. By faith he has thrown himself into the breach. He has accepted the Great Commission of Christ and by faith has chosen to help (Board for Communication Services 1986, 13).

To be a world Christian requires courage to face stark reality. It demands dedication to Christ, a dedication which refuses to allow the distressing reality to continue.

2. It's impossible!

When we attempt to cram the image of 3.6 billion lost people into our minds, it is more than we can fathom. Great is the temptation to surrender and conclude "It can't be done! It's just impossible to preach Christ to all the world!"

Many Christians have fallen prey to such thinking. For a time they are moved by the great need and challenge of reaching the lost. But after a while a sense of hopelessness, perhaps accompanied by a cloud of depression, sets in. The burden grows so heavy that these Christians begin to look for other tasks that seem more manageable. They rationalize their flagging interest in world evangelization: "Why wear myself out on a job that can never be completed? Christ must have been deluded to think it was possible."

The question to ask, however, is "Who is deluded, we or Christ?" Jesus never even hinted at the possibility that the Great Commission was unattainable. "It all comes down to: Either Christ was deceived in believing that the job can be done, or we are deceived in believing that it cannot" (Fenton 1973, 63). We tend to be fearful and doubtful when we think of the billions that need to hear the gospel. Do we have the forces to reach the world for Christ? "It can be demonstrated mathematically that all of our Lord's churches in the Western world, and all of His rising churches in the Third World, these put together can get the evangel-*ization* job *done*" (Board for Communication Services 1986, 6).

Professor C. Peter Wagner of Fuller Seminary in Pasadena estimates that less than 1 percent of believers have the gift of being able to live in another culture and be a missionary. This may seem low, but it is sufficient to do the job (Wagner 1983, 68). According to the U.S. Center for World Missions, approximately 200 million Christians in this world are seriously concerned about sharing Christ with others. If one out of every 200 were to become a cross-cultural missionary, this would provide one million mission reenforcements. With that force we would have one worker for every five thousand unreached persons (Bryant 1985, 44).

The statistics indicate that there would be sufficient missionary personnel to reach the whole world *if* the church would mobilize all its forces for that purpose. When a war of the magnitude of World War II is being waged, you don't win by playing at it. To win you must mobilize all your forces and utilize all the resources and citizenry of your land. The spiritual war against Satan and the unbelieving world will require even more dedication and concentration of effort. But the war can be won.

Who else is on our side? Why God Himself with His powerful, life-giving Word and Sacraments! Trusting in Him, we can persevere against all obstacles and win. One last frustration calls for our attention.

3. I can't save the world

When faced with the teeming millions of Christless people, many Christians have responded, "The numbers boggle my mind. What can I do? I want to help, but I can't save the whole world. I can't even save a thousand.''

Folks who think like this react in one of two ways. Most become so burdened that they just give up. Others burn themselves out, driven by an inflated sense of personal responsibility. But the world Christian need not fall into either of these traps.

Answer this: How many people has God ordered you to lead to faith in the Savior? A million, a thousand, or ten? The Lord never said, did He?

Surely, God wants all people to be saved, but He never handed you a Superman costume and ordered you to save them all. Rather, He calls you to fulfill a one-person-sized role in the vast spiritual war in which we are engaged. Although there were some outstanding heroes in World War II, it was not won by a handful of crack commandos. On the contrary, victory resulted from the efforts of millions of soldiers, sailors, pilots, marines, and supporting civilians who were faithfully at their posts day after day and obeyed the commands of their superiors with a "Yes, sir!"

In the same way, God wants you, and every Christian, to do what one faithful soldier can do, not to do the work of a whole battalion. This is a liberating concept. Even though the Great Commission is a mammoth undertaking without equal, God merely calls you to do a you-sized job. When you grasp this fact, the frustration dissolves, and you are freed to be a world Christian, doing your small but significant part in the grand war effort.

What do I mean by a you-sized role? For a senior citizen in Ontario it means praying every day for missionaries in the Middle East. For a woman in Ohio it means receiving newsletters from a dozen missionaries so that she can edit a mission column in her congregation's monthly newsletter. For a man in Dallas it means patrolling inner-city streets one night a week to minister to runaways, drug addicts, and prostitutes. For a housewife in Seattle it means cooking meals at the Seamen's Center for foreign seamen who come to port. Do you catch the implication of these examples? You don't have to go overseas to be a world Christian. You don't have to become a full-time overseas missionary to be a supporter of world evangelization.

When each of us plays a one-person-sized role, God the Holy Spirit coordinates our efforts with those of other like-minded believers. He sees that the amazingly vast battle plan is brought to completion. The mission challenge that confronted Al and confronts us is really not our challenge at all. It is the Holy Spirit's challenge. He is the field marshal; we are His forces. Though the task before us may boggle our minds, it does not boggle His in the least. He has been orchestrating the campaign for thousands of years. He still does it today.

Liberated from the Superman complex, you can toss the leotards and cape into the trash and pull on the comfortable work overalls of the average world Christian.

The Guilt That Robs Us of Joy

If you are one of those rare Christians who feel no guilt because you are actively involved in living out the Great Commission, God bless you. You probably do not need the advice in this section, but it will help you understand how other believers may feel when you talk to them about God's global purposes.

Sometimes a visit from a missionary, a sermon on missions, or even a book like this one may cause people to feel guilty. By such means we come face to face with two overwhelming truths: (1) Christ died for all people and has given us the ministry of reconciliation; (2) of the 5.2 billion men, women, and children on this globe, 2.6 billion have never even heard the good news proclaimed in a way that is understandable to them.

These alarming facts may cause waves of guilt to surge in the consciences of those who listen to a mission speaker. A tidal wave of shame and regret can extinguish people's ardor to share Christ cross-culturally. In this manner, a mission festival can become a mission fizzle, with little lasting effect. People leave, promising themselves never to think very deeply about missions again, because their consciences become immersed in remorse.

If the Great Commission leaves you feeling accused, may I suggest that you examine your guilt, rather than simply ignore it. Identifying the cause of your guilt feelings will help you deal with them more realistically. As you read the following list, consider which kind (or kinds) of guilt might be disturbing you.

1. Guilt Due to Ignorance

Some do little or nothing to support worldwide Christian outreach because they have been led to believe that the task is almost completed. They think that the gospel has been preached to almost every creature. Once such ignorance is exposed, the proper response is not to bemoan past inactivity forever, but to "take the task he gives you gladly; Let his work your pleasure be" (*Lutheran Worship*, 318, stanza 4).

2. Guilt Due to Rebellious Disobedience

Some Christians experience pangs of guilt because they have consciously chosen to ignore their Savior's command to make disciples of all nations. They are modern-day Jonahs. Jonah was called by God to warn the cruel, pagan inhabitants of Nineveh to repent of their sin or their city would be destroyed in 40 days. Rather than journey east to Nineveh, Jonah caught the first ship headed west. Now *that* is rebellious disobedience.

Why did Jonah run? Although God loved the Ninevites, Jonah hated them, because their brutal armies had conquered many peoples, including the northern tribes of Israel. With the help of the great fish, the Lord convinced Jonah to go through with His plan. He preached to the Ninevites. The Spirit led them to repent, and they were saved from God's wrath. A happy ending, right? Not for Jonah. Even though he had complied with God's command, he was still defiant and disobedient at heart, grumbling and growling at God for having spared his arch enemies. The poet Thomas Carlisle ably depicts the confrontation of wills with which the story of Jonah closes:

> And Jonah stalked
> to his shaded seat
> and waited for God
> to come around
> to his way of thinking.
>
> And God is still waiting
> for a host of Jonahs
> in their comfortable homes
> to come around
> to His way of loving.
> (Carlisle 1968, 64)

Ask yourself if this is the cause of your guilt—out and out disobedience to the Great Commission, because of dislike of and prejudice toward people of another culture. This may be hard to admit to yourself and to God; but if you will repent of this sin, the Holy Spirit will enable you to love both the people at the ends of the earth and the folks next door.

3. Guilt Due to Apathy about the Lost

Many Christians are not so openly antagonistic as Jonah. They do not hate foreigners; they simply are unconcerned about them. Their attitude is like that of the tourist who goes on an overseas vacation. With his fully automatic 35mm camera strapped around his neck, he captures all of the exotic scenery: the plants, the animals, the buildings, and the people. But notice that the people are treated like things, just part of the scenery. This tourist fails to see "the natives" as real people with emotions, burdens, trials, and dreams. He fails to see them as people who desperately need to be reconciled to their Creator.

Analyze your attitude toward the people in this world who do not know Christ. Are you apathetic about their plight? Do your guilty feelings stem from the fact that you simply do not care much about them? Apathy is sin. Apathy is simply a fancy word for lovelessness. If God were apathetic, the Bible would say, "God was so unconcerned about the world that He never bothered to give His only begotten Son; therefore everyone will perish without hope of eternal life." You know what it really says: "God so loved the world that he gave his one and only Son, that whoever believes in him shall not perish but have eternal life" (John 3:16).

4. Guilt Due to Universalistic Beliefs

Universalism is the misplaced hope that somehow or other God will simply ignore men's sins and allow everyone to be saved, whether they repent and trust in Christ or not. Others hold a moderate position, claiming that those who sincerely follow the tenets of their own religion will be pardoned by God. Either belief implies that there is no need for Christians to cross cultural barriers and proclaim justification by grace through faith in Christ.

Universalism sounds so loving, so kind. There is only one thing wrong with it. It is the exact opposite of what the Bible says:

> Multitudes who sleep in the dust of the earth will awake: some to everlasting life, others to shame and everlasting contempt. Those who are wise will shine like the brightness of the heavens, and those who lead many to righteousness, like the stars forever and ever (Dan. 12:2–3).

Those who are wise do not deny the Scriptures' teaching about eternal destruction. Rather, they lead many to the righteousness of Christ by proclaiming His name to the nations.

Who in the Bible talks the most about hell? Is it Moses, the giver of the Law? No. Is it one of the prophets whose words of warning resound through the pages of the Old Testament? No. The one who speaks the lion's share of Biblical warnings about hell is none other than Jesus Christ (See Matt. 13:36–43; 25:31–46). He who saves us from eternal death is the one who sounds the alarm most urgently.

If there really is no danger of hell, then Christ is as sadistic as the person who shouts "Fire!" in a crowded theater when there is no fire. But what if there is a fire? Then people must be alerted! Jesus does just that, pointing to the only escape route: "I am the way and the truth and the life. No one comes to the Father except through me" (John 14:6). We who have come to the Father through Christ cannot deny to others the opportunity to make the same pilgrimage of faith.

Has the lie of universalism crept into your thinking about missions? Is this the sin that troubles your conscience when you hear Christ say (Luke 24:47) that we are to preach repentance and the forgiveness of sins in His name to all nations?

5. Guilt Due to Myopic Self-Interest

Many believers who value the gospel and promote evangelism, still have difficulty seeing beyond the city limits. Suffering from the Mr. Magoo mentality about missions, they rationalize: "Yes, cross-cultural work is important, but there is so much that needs to be done right here in our community and country. We need to proclaim the Gospel more here before we concentrate on faraway places. After all, an unsaved person in North America is just as lost as an unbeliever in Morocco or Burma."

The last sentence is a half-truth. Yes, a man or woman who does not trust in Christ for salvation is lost, no matter on what piece of real estate he or she is standing. However, if a Christian thinks that the gospel is as available to a Moroccan or a Burmese as to most North Americans, nothing could be farther from the truth. For instance, the North African nation of Morocco, with a population of over twenty-four million, is 99.6 percent Muslim, 0.25 percent Roman Catholic, and 0.01 percent Protestant. Furthermore, four-tenths of that tiny sliver of Protestants are foreigners living in Morocco (Johnstone 1986, 303).

Burma, in southeast Asia, does not fare much better. Eighty-seven percent of the 37 million inhabitants are Buddhists, while Christianity weighs in at a mere 5.9 percent. Significantly, only one out of 50 Burmese Christians is from the dominant people group, the Bhama, who comprise nearly two-thirds of the population. Hats off, however, to the one thousand Burmese missionaries, most of them from the Burma Baptist Convention, who are striving to bring in a harvest from this divided and troubled land (Johnstone 1986, 122-23).

In comparison, the English-speaking world enjoys an abundance of Christian resources:

> 90% of the world's ordained ministers work among the 9% who speak English. . . .
> There is more evangelical literature printed in English than in all the other languages of the world combined (Watkins 1987c, 200).

Christ shed His blood for all nations. Let us not treat Him as a tribal god whose power and salvation are effective only for one people—ourselves. Is this the cause of your guilt? Have you set priorities for yourself and your church that only emphasize outreach to those who are like yourselves? If so, you would do well to imagine the following situation (Watkins 1968, 21). Picture 20 people carrying a heavy log. Nineteen are lifting one end, and one lone fellow is groping, straining, and struggling at the other end. Then all 20 call out to you, "Help!" Now, where will you lend a hand?

Jesus Himself recognized the varied levels of opportunity to hear the gospel and carried out His ministry accordingly. Even though His major assignment was to proclaim the good news to the lost sheep of Israel, in what region did the Savior carry out most of His ministry? It was in Galilee of the Gentiles, the part of Judea where the Jewish religion was the weakest, the place that had a high Gentile population and was surrounded by Gentile peoples. He let His light shine in the darkest place available to Him, thus fulfilling the prophecy: "The people walking in darkness have seen a great light; on those living in the land of the shadow of death a light has dawned" (Is. 9:2).

Remember your Sunday school days. One of the favorite songs was "This Little Gospel Light." When you sang, "All around the neighborhood I'm going to let it shine," how big did you imagine the neighborhood to be? Probably pretty small. In Paul's great chapter on love, he says, "When I became a man, I put childish ways behind me" (1 Cor. 13:11). Jesus said that the field is the world (Matt. 13:38). He said that our neighbor is anyone to whom we show mercy. Lay aside childish self-interest and ask God to cause your light to shine also in the dark and distant corners of the earth.

6. Guilt Due to Sins of Omission

A good number of Christians realize that the field is the whole world. They want to play a part in their Savior's Great Commission. But somehow or other their interest became derailed. Amid the hurry-skurry of life their priorities are rearranged, so that other matters drain their time, energies, and resources.

The factors that force world evangelization to the back burner are not all bad. Conscientious parents devote time and energy to their children. Christians get a new job or start a business, and they allow it to bite giant chunks out of their schedule. A congregation starts or expands a parochial school, and suddenly the members no longer contribute as much to mission work. Sometimes the vast array of church activities so consumes our time that little or nothing is left for addressing the plight of the unreached masses. Mission activist David Bryant calls this situation "smorgasborditis." The overabundance of Christian programs, books, magazines, music, and the like causes us to focus all our attention on the offerings and opportunities right in our own parish while overlooking the fact that many peoples are starving for the Word of God (Bryant 1985, 51-52).

Think about how you use your time, energy, and resources. Have you been giving God's global task a priority lower than it deserves? Perhaps this is the cause of the guilt you sense.

7. Guilt Due to Inflated Expectations

This kind of guilt is not the result of personal sin. Rather, some Christians carry a load of guilt because they assume, "If I am not a missionary, then I am failing God." In some cases this guilt may be real, if the person is running from God's call, as Jonah did. On the other hand, many people mistakenly assume that the only ones who truly obey the Great Commission are those who do cross-cultural ministry in a distant land. This is a myth. Those who energetically support missions are also fulfilling Christ's command. Furthermore, in almost every part of North America, there are opportunities to share the good news with neighbors from other ethnic backgrounds. Later chapters will demonstrate how you can participate actively in the Great Commission without ever changing your address.

I hope the list above has helped you identify the guilt that you may sense when you consider the Bible's challenge to proclaim Christ's name to the ends of the earth. But what do you do with it now?

Let God's Law and Gospel Do Their Work

In most cases, the reason that we feel guilty is that we *are* guilty. God's Law accuses us. With remorse we admit that our mission zeal fizzles because of our lack of love for Christ and for our fellow men. God thundered from Mount Sinai, "You shall not murder," and we are reminded of how we have failed to bring the Word of Life to the spiritually dead. Jesus commanded, "Love your neighbor as yourself," and we lament that we have loved ourselves much more. This is the Law that accuses us. If we have not obeyed it, our guilty hearts may be so overburdened that we cannot rise to take up the joyful challenge of God's mission.

Being cut to the heart by the Law, what will you do? Why not repent of this sin, just as you would any other? Trust in Christ's blood to cleanse you of your guilt. Call on the Holy Spirit to make the necessary changes in your heart and life. Only then can you serve Him without fear in holiness and righteousness before Him all your days (Luke 1:74–75).

If the Great Commission leaves you guilt-stricken, remember that your Savior also died for the Christian's sin of lovelessness toward the unsaved. Confess your disobedience to God. He will have mercy on you! He will freely pardon. The Holy Spirit will grant you His strength to amend your selfish ways and learn to love all people.

How can you know this is true? The Bible affirms it in the words of the apostle John:

> My dear children, I write this to you so that you will not sin. But if anybody does sin, we have one who speaks to the Father in our defense— Jesus Christ, the Righteous One. He is the atoning sacrifice for our sins, and not only for ours but also for the sins of the whole world (1 John 2:1– 2).

In addition, the Bible affirms it in the real life example of the apostle John. When John wrote the above words about forgiveness, he was not merely theorizing. John himself had been guilty of the sin of despising the lost. He himself had experienced God's merciful pardon even for this sin. Here's the story:

> As the time approached for him to be taken up to heaven, Jesus resolutely set out for Jerusalem. And he sent messengers on ahead, who went into a Samaritan village to get things ready for him; but the people there did not welcome him, because he was heading for Jerusalem. When the disciples James and John saw this, they asked, "Lord, do you want us to call fire down from heaven to destroy them?" But Jesus turned and rebuked them, and they went to another village (Luke 9:51–56).

Fire of judgment from heaven! That was all that John and his brother thought this Samaritan village deserved. The mercy of God was the farthest thing from their minds. Instead, they were driven by the ethnic prejudice which the Jews harbored against the Samaritans.

Jesus rebuked James and John for their vindictive proposal. To our minds

41

that simple rebuke might not seem enough—a mere slap on the wrist. Why didn't He strip them of their rank of apostle and put more worthy men in their places? You may wonder the same thing regarding yourself: "After all my failures to take His Great Commission seriously, how could Christ ever use me now to bring His gospel to the nations?"

Now hear the rest of the story. Acts 8 relates how, a few years later, Philip the Deacon was proclaiming Christ in the land of Samaria. Until then the apostles had been slow to bring the gospel to foreigners such as the Samaritans. Receiving word of conversions among the Samaritans, the Twelve sent two of their number, Peter and John, to check into the matter. When they arrived and prayed for the Samaritan converts, something astounding happened. They received the Holy Spirit.

Imagine how John felt. Previously, he had wanted to call down fire on a Samaritan village. His goal was judgment and wrath. Now God used him to call down another fire from heaven, the Holy Spirit, the fire of forgiveness, rebirth, and renewal.

Christ did not reject John as an apostle! Neither will He reject you!

"Peter and John returned to Jerusalem, preaching the gospel in many Samaritan villages" (Acts 8:25). The text does not tell us which villages they went to, but it is altogether possible that John said, "Peter, there is one village in particular that I want to visit, the one that James and I wanted to see burned to the ground. What a loveless fool I was then! With all my heart I long to go to that village now and tell them about the loving Savior they previously rejected."

This is how John's mission failure was transformed into a mission festival. The joy of God's pardoning love overcame John's guilt and fears. Any doubts that he was an unworthy instrument were overruled by the joy of being used by Christ to proclaim His name to those in darkness.

The same is true for you. Confessing your mission sins to God, there is no doubt that the blood of Jesus Christ purifies you of all sin and guilt. You are free to enjoy a lifetime of mission activity. Be assured that the Holy Spirit will indeed empower you to contribute to the Triune God's ultimate goal for mankind:

> "My name will be great among the nations, from the rising to the setting of the sun. In every place incense and pure offerings will be brought to my name, because my name will be great among the nations," says the Lord Almighty (Mal. 1:11).

The Burden for the Lost

In this chapter we have confronted two factors, frustration and guilt, that often hinder a Christian's participation in Great Commission activities. I hope the foregoing discussions have caused these obstacles to dwindle in size. Perhaps a chat with a pastor or some other Christian will help you deal with whatever difficulties remain.

However, many readers will probably have one more concern that weighs heavily on them. "Okay," they may say, "I understand now that I don't have to be frustrated by the Great Commission, because God only expects me to do a me-sized part of the work. And even though I have not done as much as I could have in the past, I thank God for giving me a new start in Christ. But still there is a burden that remains: the responsibility that I have (along with all other Christians) to see that Christ is shared with people who do not know His glorious, saving name. That knowledge weighs me down."

If that is how you feel, you have a point. The burden of world evangelization is still there, resting squarely on the shoulders of every redeemed child of God. I congratulate you for recognizing its presence. Many Christians do not. You see clearly the duty and charge that the Lord of glory has given us. You can relate fully to the feelings of Marilyn Laszlo, a Wycliffe Bible translator in the village of Hauna, Papua New Guinea: "As we translated and as we taught the people to read and write their own language, we became burdened for all the enemy tribes around us. Hundreds of villages were untouched" (Laszlo 1982, 213).

One day Marilyn was visited by a group of sickly people who, to reach Hauna, had paddled through the swamp four days. While these folks were being treated for their illness, they observed that people were going to school to learn how to read and write their own language. The Word of God was being proclaimed by local pastors. When the time came for the visitors to return home, the leader begged Marilyn to come to their village and write down their language so that God might speak to them too. Several weeks later Marilyn made the arduous journey and received a warm welcome from the leader. Marilyn relates the conversation that ensued:

> As we were walking through the village, I noticed in the center a new building, very different from their regular houses. I knew it had just been built and I asked, "What is that building there in the center of the village?"
> He said, "Oh, that is God's house—that's our church."
> "Your church? Do you have a mission here?"
> "Oh, no, we have never had a mission here."
> "Well, do you have a pastor here—you know, someone that comes to preach God's Word?"
> "Oh, no, we've never had a pastor here."
> "Well, is there someone here in the village that can read and write Pidgin English who holds services in your church?"
> "Oh, no! There is no one here that can read or write. And we have no books."
> I looked at him and said, "Then what is that building for?"
> He said, "Well, we saw the little church in your village and our people decided to build a church too. Now we're waiting. We're waiting for someone to come and tell us about God in our own talk, in our language."
> I turned and started crying. I have never seen that kind of faith. Friends, out in the middle of the jungle stands that little church and today they are still waiting—waiting for someone to come and tell them in their own language about Jesus (Laszlo 1982, 214–15).

If we have learned the lessons taught in this chapter, this story should not frustrate us. Nor should it make us feel guilty. But it will leave us burdened. Marilyn Laszlo wept. We world Christians can weep too, or at least feel sorrow and anguish. These are altogether wholesome and proper responses of the Christian's heart. Paul was sensing the very same burden when he wrote:

> I have great sorrow and unceasing anguish in my heart. For I could wish that I myself were cursed and cut off from Christ for the sake of my brothers, those of my own race, the people of Israel (Rom. 9:2–4).

These words follow perhaps the most majestically reassuring words in the Bible:

> For I am convinced that neither death nor life, neither angels nor demons, neither the present nor the future, nor any powers, neither height nor depth, nor anything else in all creation, will be able to separate us from the love of God that is in Christ Jesus our Lord (Rom. 8:38–39).

After these triumphant words, the contrast is shocking when Paul says, "I have great sorrow and unceasing anguish in my heart" (Rom. 9:2). What concern causes this constant flow of deep emotions? Paul's heart is wrenched by the fact that the majority of the Jews do not believe. All world Christians bear a similar burden. The sorrow and anguish you bear is your concern for the lost, whether they be Jew or Gentile.

Bending under this weight, we may complain, "So how do I get rid of it!" The answer is simple. We do not if we wish to be Christ's disciples. We cannot shrug off the burden, because Jesus Himself gave it to us. To all His disciples He said, "If anyone would come after me, he must deny himself and take up his cross and follow me" (Matt. 16:24).

Often we refer to illness or tragedies as crosses that people must bear. The Bible does not use the term in that way. *Cross* in the New Testament means the personal sacrifice and even persecution that believers endure in order that they may witness faithfully about Christ. Bearing the cross, Jesus says, entails denying ourselves, even losing our lives for the sake of the gospel.

Paul gives us a marvelous example of this sacrificial attitude in the impassioned words quoted earlier: "For I could wish that I myself were cursed and cut off from Christ for the sake of my brothers, those of my own race, the people of Israel"(Rom. 9:3). Paul knew, of course, that he could not really die to save the unbelieving Jews. So instead he chose to die for them day by day, bit by bit, by bringing the message of Christ to Jew and Gentile alike, as God gave him opportunity. On another occasion, Paul described his cross as his very reason for living: "I consider my life worth nothing to me, if only I may finish the race and complete the task the Lord Jesus has given me—the task of testifying to the gospel of God's grace" (Acts 20:24).

Today, God calls us to bear our crosses in a variety of innovative ways. Some do so by dedicating twenty minutes a day to pray for missionaries and national believers in a particular country. Others assume the challenge of giving 10 percent of their income to finance the many demands of world missions. Some are led by the Holy Spirit to take up the task of serving Christ in a distant land. Others learn Spanish or another language, in order to serve the ethnic elements in their own neighborhood.

Perhaps you feel unequal to the task. Perhaps you fear that you will buckle beneath the burden of world evangelization. Fear not! You carry none of these responsibilities alone. God makes the burden light. Jesus said so: "Take my yoke upon you and learn from me, for I am gentle and humble in heart, and you will find rest for your souls. For my yoke is easy and my burden is light" (Matt. 11:29–30). Perhaps you have cherished this promise when you faced some difficulty. Now recognize how it provides the under-girding strength you need to bear the burden-cross of world evangelization. "Praise be to the Lord, to God our Savior, who daily bears our burdens" (Ps. 68:19).

In this chapter we have learned that God gladly lifts mission frustrations and guilt from our weary backs. But the cross He will not remove. The Lord wants to bless you with great sorrow and unceasing anguish for the lost. That sounds crazy, does it not? In our look-out-for-Number-One society, great sorrow and unceasing anguish are not sought-after experiences.

For us to shoulder this burden willingly, we need to recognize what sorrow and anguish are. They are love, sacrificial love, Christ-like love. The world Christian only takes up his cross of great sorrow and unceasing anguish be-cause by faith he knows that his Savior came to earth motivated by His own sorrow and anguish over our lost condition. Jesus expressed these profound emotions in Gethsemane the night before He died: "My soul is overwhelmed with sorrow to the point of death. Stay here and keep watch with me" (Matt. 26:38). By bearing the same sorrow (though on a far smaller scale), we continue to "keep watch" with Him. We bear our crosses because He bore His. We lay down our lives because He laid down His.

We are not the first ones to bear the cross of mission work. Previous generations of world Christians provide us with inspiring examples. We shall be cheered and emboldened by their example in the next chapter.

Something Now

1. *Search Scripture.* Read the book of Jonah as though you had never heard it before. On a sheet of paper make two columns: one to jot down words and actions that reveal Jonah's attitude toward the heathen, another to record God's words and actions. Compare the two columns. Compare your words and actions regarding world evangelization to those of Jonah and the Lord.

2. *Read.* Obtain (from the LCMS) the little booklet "Personal World Missionary Strategy." Carry it with you. Use it to jot down your observations about being a world Christian and your you-sized role in the mission of God.

3. *Listen* to the song "Asleep in the Light" by Keith Green. Ponder the lyrics. How applicable is this song to you and to your congregation? Have you been asleep in the light? Don't overlook the closing lines. Who is speaking these words? In contrast to the strong Law emphasis of the rest of the song, what Gospel hope do the closing lines give to those who wish to awake from their slumber?

4. *Look.* The next time you view a mission-related movie, filmstrip, or slide show, ask yourself: How did this presentation leave me feeling? Was I only accused by the Law or also motivated by the Gospel of Christ? Was I encouraged to seek the Holy Spirit's strength to meet the mission challenges before me?

5. *Converse.* Share your honest feelings about missions with someone you trust. Include the negative feelings as well as positive ones. Allow others opportunity to speak in return, and listen with care.

6. *Pray.* For seven days use Romans 9:1–3 and 10:1 as a guide during your private prayer time. Ponder why Paul used such strong terms as "great sorrow," "unceasing anguish," and "heart's desire." Ask the Holy Spirit to reveal to you the full meaning of these phrases.

Chapter 4

The Heritage of Joy

To bring Christ's joy to the entire world is not a new project just recently voted into being by resolution of a church convention. It is not merely the stepchild of Western expansion and colonialism. Nor is it simply a frantic, statistical pipe dream inspired by the approach of the year 2000. On the contrary, God's mission has always been with us. It is a holy enterprise with a broad and brave history. It is a perpetual relay race in which the baton of the cross has been passed from land to land and from generation to generation. If you trust in Christ as your Savior, you are now running a leg of that race; the baton is in your hand. To whom will you pass it on?

Your joy and effectiveness in the race will be increased by learning about the heritage of missions. Therefore, this chapter will offer you a brief summary of mission history. Some readers may receive this news with a weary yawn because they have always found history dull and laborious. Before you flip ahead to the next chapter, please consider one fact: The Lord "is not the God of the dead but of the living" (Matt. 22:32). Therefore, every missionary of the past, every Christian who promoted cross-cultural evangelism, and every convert who then led others to the Redeemer—they are all still alive. Those who carried the gospel from place to place are living with the Lord in Paradise. And someday we shall meet them there!

This is why the story of world evangelization cannot be dry, stodgy history. We rejoice in earlier victories because we are runners in the same race. We continue to fight in the same crucial clash between God and Satan, life and death, light and darkness. This warfare is not one that conquers and oppresses people, as is so common in human history. The advancing forces of Christ liberate dying men, women, and children from the oppressive power of sin, death, and the devil.

Surely there is no greater enterprise in history. To rehearse the earlier chapters of the struggle and expansion of the gospel is to sense the rich heritage of which we are a part. In all likelihood, you have already appreciated this richness while singing "Lift High the Cross," "Stand Up, Stand Up For Jesus," and "For All the Saints."

If such hymns have made your heart beat faster and your faith swell with the desire to proclaim Him who bought you with His blood, then you have already tasted the heady wine of mission heritage. May the following summary

47

provide you a full draft of this "wine that gladdens the heart" of Christians (Ps. 104:15).

Old Testament Missions (Creation to A.D. 30)

Most Christians assume that missions began with Christ's pronouncement of the Great Commission and the Holy Spirit's display of power on Pentecost. However, God's worldwide plan of redemption began long before that. We see His plan as early as the first gospel promise in Gen. 3:15: "And I will put enmity between you and the woman, and between your offspring and hers; he will crush your head, and you will strike his heel." Mission historian W. G. Polack observed:

> Adam and Eve, as the parents of the whole human race, received the promise of a Savior for all men. The supposition that the Promised One was to redeem only a part, one race or family, out of the mass of humanity, was excluded at the outset (Polack 1930, 3).

When God called Abraham to establish the Jewish nation, He promised "all peoples on earth will be blessed through you" (Gen. 12:3). God's purpose was to create a nation which lived so close to Him, that all peoples would be attracted to that nation (Deut. 26:18–19). This purpose reached its pinnacle in the early reign of King Solomon who "was greater in riches and wisdom than all the other kings of the earth. The whole world sought audience with Solomon to hear the wisdom God put in his heart" (1 Kings 10:23–24). Details are provided in 1 Kings 10:1–13 regarding the visit of one of those dignitaries, the Queen of Sheba. But then disaster struck. Though Solomon was a wise man, he turned out to be an old fool, for his "seven hundred wives of royal birth . . . led him astray. As Solomon grew old, his wives turned his heart after other gods, and his heart was not fully devoted to the Lord his God" (1 Kings 11:3–4). Solomon built places of worship for these idols on the southern end of the Mount of Olives, across the valley from the temple of Jehovah. With this development, Israel's golden era became tarnished. The rest of Old Testament history is a tug-of-war between wayward Jews bent on worshipping false gods and prophets sent to call them back to the living God.

By the time of Christ, God had made His people as numerous as the stars in the sky, and their influence was felt in far-flung regions:

> The witness of the Jews was extensive. They were scattered into Babylon, Syria, Asia Minor, and other parts of the Tigris-Euphrates valley, Egypt, and North Africa. Historians estimate that about seven percent of the people in areas around the Mediterranean were Jews. Many pagan people became followers of the Jewish faith (Syrdal 1967, 31).

During this long era, God was indeed beginning to fulfill His promise: "For as the soil makes the sprout come up and a garden causes seeds to grow, so the Sovereign Lord will make righteousness and praise spring up before all nations" (Is. 61:11).

The Apostolic Era (A.D. 30 to 100)

Dr. Ed Westcott, Missouri Synod executive secretary of the Board for Mission Services, enjoys imagining the anxiety the apostles may have felt when left behind on the mount of ascension. The Lord had ordered them to take the gospel to all nations, but they were only twelve men. They had no budget. They had no strategy. They had no mission board and no organizational chart. What did they have? Only what we have: the assurance that they were "justified freely by his grace through the redemption that came by Christ Jesus" (Rom. 3:24). Therefore, they could not help speaking about what they had seen and heard (Acts 4:20).

In the book of Acts, proclaiming Christ was the primary activity of the apostolic church. Everyone, not only the apostles, was quick to share the life-giving faith. When the chief priests and elders countered with persecution, the believers prayed. They did not pray for the persecution to be lifted; they asked God to enable His servants to speak His Word with boldness (Acts 4:29). The Lord did enable them. And they did speak boldly. When the heat of persecution led all but the apostles to evacuate Jerusalem, personal evangelism did not falter because "those who had been scattered preached the word wherever they went" (Acts 8:4).

Acts concentrates on the exploits of Peter in Palestine and Paul in Cyprus, Turkey, Greece, and Rome. Christian tradition informs us where the others served:

> John: Jerusalem, and later Ephesus and eastern Turkey.
> Andrew: Greece and the regions beyond the Black Sea.
> Matthew: Ethiopia.
> Bartholomew: Armenia (western Turkey) and possibly India.
> Philip: central Turkey.
> Judas Thaddaeus: Arabia, Syria, and Persia.
> Simon the Zealot: North Africa, as far as Morocco.
> James, the son of Alphaeus: Spain.
> Thomas: Odessa, Persia, and India. The present day "Thomas Christians" on the Malabar Coast of India claim Thomas as their founder (Syrdal 1967, 52 and Polack 1930, 14).

Although our information about most of the apostles is fragmentary, no doubt they had adventures as dramatic as those of Peter and Paul. We will hear the details in heaven. Clearly, these twelve men and the hosts of other believers made a monumental impact on the world of their time. Would that we who have mission boards and budgets were as dedicated as they to the church's primary task!

The Post-Apostolic Era (A.D. 100 to 313)

This was a period marked by repeated persecutions of the believers, until Christianity became the state religion of the Roman Empire in 313. In spite of the machinations of Satan and godless men, the church grew through the Christians' bold witness to their friends—and even to their persecutors.

> Many a time in the long night-watches, when a soldier had been chained to a Christian in order to guard him, the two would have a conversation, and the Christian would tell the soldier of the wonderful joy which had come into his life when he became a follower of Jesus. In this way many soldiers were won for the Savior, and there grew up, inside the Roman army, groups of these men who were Christians. As these soldiers then were sent to the various parts of the great Roman Empire, they carried the message of Christ into every country and province where they went, so that, as the years passed, practically every city and every town in the Mediterranean world came to have a group of men and women in its midst who had been won for Christ (Polack 1930, 17).

Evangelism was also carried out on an intellectual level by the Apologists who in their writings and their schools of philosophy defended the Christian faith against pagan philosophies. One of the Apologists, named Origen, compared witnessing Christians to arrows. Origen's zeal to be an arrow for God was fulfilled as he led people to Christ in his school of philosophy. One such person was Gregory, an upper-class young man from northern Turkey, who met Origen while journeying to Beirut where he planned to study rhetoric and law. Gregory never made it to Beirut, but at the feet of Origen he learned the way to heaven. Gregory later wrote about his conversion, saying that Origen's words had pierced him like arrows. "How fascinating that Origen's own prayer that he should be one of God's arrows was so signally granted in the case of this young convert!" (Green 1970, 228).

A Step Forward, a Step Back (A.D. 313 to 1517)

During these twelve centuries advances were made in some areas but were accompanied by losses in other regions of the world. The greatest step forward was the evangelization of Europe. At the beginning of this era only the southern part of the continent had heard the good news; by the end of the 14th century all of Europe was to some degree Christian, Lithuania being the last stronghold of paganism to fall (Neill 1964, 111–12).

The greatest step backward was the loss of North Africa and the Middle East to Islam. This religion, founded by Mohammed in A.D. 622, was considered the church's archenemy. In Muslim lands, conversion to Christianity was punishable by death (and it still is in some countries). As a result the means of "converting" Muslims was often the sword and not the Word of God. Multitudes of knights were willing to shed their blood in the Crusades, the military attempts to free the Holy Land from Muslim rule (1095–1291).

In contrast, only a handful of courageous disciples, (e.g., Robert Lull [1235–1315]) were willing to learn Arabic, journey to Muslim lands, and preach Christ to the people. Perhaps the greatest witness to Muslims during this era was given by Christians who became enslaved to Muslims. Only in eternity shall we hear the unrecorded adventures of these slaves who led some of their Muslim masters to the Master, Jesus Christ.

Lutheran readers may be interested to know how the ancestors of the first Lutheran lands came to hear of Christ. Germany was evangelized by missionaries from England, the most prominent being Boniface (A.D. 680–755), the "Apostle of Germany" who challenged Thor, the god of thunder, by cutting down an oak tree consecrated to him. When no lightning bolts fell, awestruck nations were convinced of the reality and power of the Christian God. At 85, Boniface was still preaching the Gospel in the Netherlands.

Other English and Irish missionaries (usually monks) brought the light of the Gospel to many European peoples. Norway is an example where Olaf Tryggvesson, a Viking raider in his youth, became a Christian and eventually king of Norway. As king, he attempted to convert all Norway to Christianity by forcing people to be baptized or be killed (Syrdal 1967, 89).

While not condoning his "evangelism" method, today Norway is one of the greatest per capita contributors of missionaries in the world. There are 1,539 Norwegian missionaries spreading the joy of Christ's salvation in 44 lands. This is a ratio of one missionary for every 2,600 Norwegian Protestants. In addition, there are about fourteen thousand groups of Norwegian believers actively supporting those who have been sent into the field (Johnstone 1986, 329–30). Cheers for Norway! Praise to the Lord of the harvest!

Mission work also occurred in more far-flung corners of the world. We know that Christian missionaries reached China in the seventh century, but the church they established dwindled by the year 1000. Again in the thirteenth century, missionaries sent by the pope made contact with the great conquerors Genghis Khan and Kublai Khan. When they arrived they found that some of the Mongol rulers' wives and also leading court officials were Christians (Neill 1964, 120). Indeed, the faith had not died out. Faithful, anonymous witnesses had kept it alive down through the centuries.

The Reformation Era (1517-1580)

During this period northern Europe experienced what might be called a "re-evangelization." In a continent that had become bogged down in human traditions and work-righteousness, the Reformers pointed troubled souls to the gospel truths Protestants hold dear: salvation through grace alone, by Christ alone, through faith alone—a message found in Scripture alone. "In fact, Luther and his disciples were fairly submerged in the mightiest missionary undertaking since the days of the apostles. They had to instruct the 'heathen' who were at the very door-steps" (Polack 1930, 39).

The Reformation was truly an international mission event. From 1520 to

1560, sixteen thousand theological students attended Wittenberg University. One-third of these students came from other lands (Bunkowske 1985, 170). "When Luther gave back to the world the Bible, the source of all true faith and Christian service, he laid the foundation for all the Protestant missionary movements that came after him" (Polack 1930, 43).

Although most of the Protestant churches' efforts went to revitalizing the European church, mission work among non-Christians was not totally overlooked. King Gustavus Vasa (1496–1560) of Sweden encouraged work among the pagan Lapps and had the New Testament translated into their language. Luther urged the proclamation of the gospel of Christ to the Jews of Germany and the Turks (Muslims) of the Balkans. Primus Truber (1506—86) and Baron Ungnad von Sonegg (1493–1564) did just that, establishing missions to the southern Slavs and the Turks (Bunkowske 1985, 170–72).

Mission work to Turks is still urgent today. In fact, Turkey is the world's largest unevangelized nation. In a population of 52 million there are only 250 converts from Islam (Johnstone 1986, 414–15). Isn't it time that the spiritual descendants of Luther eagerly take up the challenge that he urged and prayed about nearly five centuries ago?

The Slow Start of Protestant Missions (1580–1792)

From 1500 to 1800, Roman Catholic mission work flourished as never before. The New World and the passage to the Far East were discovered by dauntless explorers from Catholic lands. Catholic missionaries soon followed, in particular those of the Society of Jesus, also known as the Jesuit Order, founded by Ignatius Loyola in 1534. "Within the next hundred years Jesuits were to lay their bones in almost every country of the known world and on the shores of almost every sea" (Neill 1964, 148). The most famous of these men was Francis Xavier (1506–52), who served in India and Japan.

Meanwhile, Protestants were doing precious little mission work. For this failure there were some reasonable explanations.

1. The Protestant Church had to expend manpower and resources to defend its very existence. The Thirty Years War (1618–48), which threatened to restore papal rule by force of arms, devastated and crippled the Protestant lands.

2. Foreign lands were inaccessible to the evangelicals. In the sixteenth century, Spain and Portugal ruled the seas and established colonies all over the world; Protestant countries were forbidden entry to them.

Nevertheless, after the Protestant lands had secured their existence militarily, and after England and Holland had become maritime and colonial powers, Protestant mission work should have surged forward. Unfortunately, the surge was slow in coming. Why? First of all, spiritual fervor was on the wane in many Protestant churches. Where faith in Christ has become mechanical and the joy of salvation has waned, mission zeal succumbs to a malady we could call "hardening of the hearteries." The first step toward mission action is always to heighten personal awareness of sin and salvation, through the preaching of Law and Gospel.

Secondly, mission interest was weakened, because some pastors and theologians taught that the Great Commission had been intended only for the twelve apostles and therefore disclaimed any present-day responsibility to reach the lost. Many of their listeners lethargically accepted this faulty interpretation and did next to nothing to further the cause of Christ to the ends of the earth. Thank God, not everyone succumbed to the anesthesia (Polack 1930, 49–56 and Scherer 1987, 66–70)!

King Gustavus Adolphus of Sweden (1594–1632) renewed and revitalized the Lapland mission begun by Gustavus Vasa. John Companius preached to the Delaware Indians in Pennsylvania. In 1660 he translated Luther's Small Catechism into their language, the first book ever translated into an American Indian tongue. The Danish-Halle Mission began work among the Tamil-speaking people of India in 1706. Through the pioneer work of men like Heinrich Pluetschau, Bartholomew Ziegenbalg, Christian Frederick Schwartz, and others, the Danish-Halle Mission established the first permanent Protestant church in Asia.

In the same period, a Norwegian man and his family devoted their lives to bringing the peace of Christ to the populace of Greenland. From 1722 to 1735 Hans Egede and his wife Gjertrud ministered to Eskimos whose hearts at first seemed more frozen than the Arctic terrain. Their work reached a tragic climax in 1733–34, when small-pox swept through the region. Of the 1200 Greenlanders who lived in Egede's community, only eight survived, and the total number of victims reached between 2,000 and 3,000. Amid the terror, Hans and Gjertrud served the dying with undaunted energy. In an age of no vaccines, their ministrations were especially heroic.

> A Greenlander who, while strong and healthy, had not cared about the instruction of the minister, nay, had even met it with derision, when dying bore witness to his goodness in the following pathetic words: "You have been more kind to us, than we have been to one another; you have fed us, when we famished; you have buried our dead, who would else have been a prey to dogs, foxes and ravens, and in particular you have told us of God and how to become blessed, so that we may now die gladly, in expectation of a better life hereafter" (Bobe 1952, 162).

Although Gjertrud survived the epidemic, her health was broken by the tragic ordeal and she entered heaven on December 21, 1734. Despondent, Hans returned home in 1735, but the following year his son Paul took up the mantle of his father. Even though Paul had hoped to be a sailor, he denied himself that ambition in order to share God's Word and Sacraments in Greenland. He proved to be a very effective missionary. Building on the foundation laid by his parents, he brought many Greenlanders to the Lord Jesus.

The examples cited thus far were only occasional lanterns in a night of general mission indifference. There was, however, one bright beacon of light: the Moravians. In a period of 150 years they sent out 2,170 missionaries. By

1950, they had three times as many souls in their overseas congregations as in their home churches (Burgess 1954, 7).

Who were the Moravians? They were a group which had campaigned for reforms in the Roman Catholic Church before the Reformation. Persecuted and driven from place to place, they finally found a permanent refuge in 1722 at the estate of Count Nicolaus Ludwig von Zinzendorf. A pious Lutheran who had resigned all his government positions in order to dedicate his whole life to the kingdom of God, Zinzendorf eventually was ordained the bishop of the Moravian settlement in 1737.

In 1731 Zinzendorf was in Copenhagen to attend the coronation of King Christian VI of Denmark. There the Count met two Eskimos who had been baptized by Egede and also a baptized black slave from the island of St. Thomas in the West Indies.

> When he returned, the account he gave of meeting these men from unevangelized lands called forth the deepest interest. . . . A visit from Anton, the slave, deepened the impression; and the account of what the slaves suffered, which they also might have to suffer, only made the fire burn more strongly. If it was difficult to approach the plantations to teach the slaves, the volunteers were ready to sell themselves as slaves to reach the poor lost souls (Murray 1979, 58).

A year later the first two missionaries left. What at first was only a trickle became a river of the water of life. In 1967, it was reported: "One out of every ninety-two members of the Moravian Church is a missionary, and at one time the ratio was one out of every sixty" (Syrdal 1967, 119).

What an example of mission dedication! Why not do some arithmetic? Take the total number of members in your home church, and divide it by 92. The quotient is the number of missionaries that your congregation would have if it sent out cross-cultural witnesses at the rate that is common in Moravian circles. It certainly gives you a goal worth praying for and striving toward. The chart below provides similar food for thought on a denominational level.

Establishing Beachheads (1792–1865)

"Attempt great things for God; expect great things of God." This was the motto of William Carey (1761–1834), the cobbler-pastor whose work marked a turning point in the history of Christian outreach. In 1792 Carey wrote a treatise entitled "An Enquiry into the Obligation of Christians to Use Means for the Conversion of the Heathens." A means came into existence soon afterward with the foundation of the Baptist Missionary Society. All the society needed was a volunteer, and Carey was their man. In June 1793 he, his wife Dolly, and their four children sailed for India. Eventually Carey and other missionaries settled in Serampore, just north of Calcutta. There they translated and printed Bibles or Scripture portions in 46 languages.

TABLE 1

RATE OF CHURCH MEMBERS PER OVERSEAS MISSIONARY

Lutheran Church Bodies	1984 Members	1985 Miss.	Ratio
Church of the Lutheran Brethren	11,006	57	193
Assoc. of Free Luth. Congs.	17,665	12	1,472
American Lutheran Church	2,339,946	310	7,548
Lutheran Church-Missouri Synod	2,631,374	310	8,477
Wisconsin Ev. Lutheran Synod	415,630	44	9,446
Lutheran Church in America	2,910,281	246	11,830

Some Other Church Bodies	1984 Members	1985 Miss.	Ratio
Brethren Assemblies (Plymouth)	98,000	554	176
Christian & Missionary Alliance	158,218	874	255
Seventh Day Adventists	638,929	1,052	607
Presbyterian Church in America	168,239	263	639
Christian Reformed Church	224,764	266	845
Church of the Nazarene	516,020	595	867
Christian Chs./Chs. of Christ	1,043,642	709	1,471
Assemblies of God	2,036,453	1,237	1,646
Baptist Bible Fellowship Int'l.	1,400,900	620	2,259
Southern Baptists	14,341,821	3,346	4,286
United Church of Christ	1,696,107	229	7,406
Presbyterian Church, USA	3,092,151	266	11,624
United Methodist Church	9,291,936	516	18,007
Episcopal Church	2,775,424	118	23,520

Source: Morris Watkins, *Seven Worlds to Win* (Fort Wayne: Great Commission Resource Library, 1987), 206.

Note: Most, if not all, of the above denominations have some members serving under interdenominational boards and others serving cross-culturally in North America.

William Carey was the first great English-speaking missionary. "The impact of his example reverberated throughout the English-speaking world, and his little book became the Magna Carta of the Protestant mission movement" (Winter 1981, 168-69). After Carey broke the logjam, more missionary societies were founded and many more soldiers of Christ advanced into realms that Satan had claimed as his own. These workers advanced with the highest of motives.

> During the nineteenth century three groups of Europeans were part of the outward thrust of the West into the East—the diplomats, the merchants, and the missionaries. . . . The missionaries were the only ones who went to give and not to get. They gave all they had—time, strength, money, love, and even life itself. . . .
>
> This is not to whitewash the missionaries. . . . They had their full share of idiosyncrasies. They had their headaches and their hang-ups. They had their doubts and their fears. Touch them, and they were touchy. Cross them, and they got cross. There were limits to their endurance (Kane 1986, 111-12).

Because of their efforts Protestant missions made great strides forward during the 1800s. Churches were established along the coasts of most of Africa and Asia.

Invading the Interiors (1865–1945)

By the latter part of the nineteenth century some people were talking as though the task of world evangelization was nearly completed. Was it? The answer was provided by missionary J. Hudson Taylor (1832–1905). After a six-year tour of duty in China, he and his wife Maria returned to England for an extended furlough. They needed time to recover from some physical ailments, to learn medicine, and to revise the Ningpo New Testament. In his spare time Hudson spoke to Christian groups about the great spiritual need of the multitudes of Chinese who lived inland, far from any missionary outpost.

> As Taylor traveled through England people were moved, not by his eloquence of speech or his impressive knowledge, but by his passion for lost souls: "A million a month dying without God," rang in the ears of his listeners, and many responded. The foundation of a great missionary society was being laid (Tucker 1983, 180).

The China Inland Mission was formed in 1865, with Taylor as its director. By 1882 this nondenominational society had workers in every province of China. How God blessed the enterprise over the years! By 1914 it was the largest foreign mission agency in the world, reaching a peak of 1,368 missionaries in 1934. Today the China Inland Mission is named the Overseas Missionary Fellowship, indicative of its ever widening activities in the Far East.

Hudson Taylor and the China Inland Mission demonstrated to the church that the work of world evangelization was far from complete. Yes, beachheads had been established, but an army only establishes a beachhead in order to invade the interior. Many churches and mission societies grasped this principle, and the gospel marched inland.

A fine example of inland penetration is the work of German missionaries in what is today Papua New Guinea. Begun by the Neuendettelsau Mission in 1886 and the Rhenish Mission in 1887, these groups overcame disease and other obstacles. Regarding the loss of so many missionaries in the early years, German missiologist G. F. Vicedom observes:

> How are the heathen to learn how a Christian behaves in times of sickness and of deep distress, if they have not seen the way in which their missionaries face such things? How can the converts learn to die as Christians should, if they have not seen in a missionary's death that the Gospel can set a man completely free from the fear of death? Even death itself can be a teacher of the Gospel (Vicedom 1961, 13).

From the outset, the goal of the Germans was to penetrate the depths of this land divided by mountain ridges, multiple languages, tribal warfare, and cannibalism. In 1908 they began to send out Papuans as missionaries to the tribes of the interior. By 1960, there was one national missionary evangelist for every 173 believers (Vicedom 1961, 45).

From 1865 to 1945, similar advances were made throughout Africa and Asia. The interior lands were being invaded by the gospel of Jesus Christ. For the first time the globe had a religion that could truly be called a "world religion"—Christianity. Was the church now on the verge of fulfilling its commission to "preach the goods news to all creation" (Mark 16:15)?

Charting the Final Assaults (1945 to 1990)

The most thrilling development of this era is the miracle that the Lord has worked in the Peoples Republic of China. Herbert Kane, who served in China from 1935 to 1950, reports from his perspective:

> When the missionaries were obliged to leave in the early 1950s, total church membership was just below the one million mark. The missionaries knew it was the end of the mission. They feared it would prove to be the end of the church as well, and the Great Proletarian Cultural Revolution (1966–69) seemed to confirm their worst fears. But the church did not die. It survived and grew at an amazing rate in recent years.
>
> With the death of Mao Zedong and the rise to power of Deng Xiaoping in 1976, China turned her face again toward the West, and we began to hear rumors of house churches springing up all over the country. The rumors, we feared, were too good to be true. There could not be *that* many Christians in China! Well, we were mistaken. Now we are told on good authority that there may be 50 million Christians in China. If that seems like an inflated figure, you can slice it in half and still have 25 million! If that figure is accurate, it represents the largest influx of new believers into the Christian church by confession of faith, any time, anywhere, in two thousand years

of church history. It is the Lord's doing and it is marvelous in our eyes (Kane 1986, 21-22).

The life-giving Word of God is working marvelous results in other regions as well, particularly in Korea, sub-Sahara Africa, and Latin America.

Furthermore, during the post-World War II era, the Holy Spirit has been raising up mission strategists whose efforts are laying the necessary groundwork to reach the whole world with the message of Christ's redemption. One of these men was Cameron Townsend (1896–1982), affectionately known as Uncle Cam.

> He grew up in California, dropped out of college, and got a job selling Spanish Bibles in Guatemala in Central America. He found out that Spanish Bibles were hard to sell in Guatemala because most people are Indians, and Indians don't usually speak Spanish. A chief of the Cakchikel tribe asked him one day, "If your God is so smart, how come He can't make a Bible in the Cakchikel language?" That did it for Cam! Nobody was going to tell him what his God couldn't do, so right then and there he started to become a Bible translator instead of a Bible seller. . . .
>
> He knew he wouldn't be able to translate the Bible into many languages by himself. So he started recruiting others. That was the start of the Wycliffe Bible Translators, now the biggest mission organization in the world with almost 5,000 workers. But translators have to be trained, so Cam and his buddies started a training school . . . . the "Summer Institute of Linguistics" (Board for Communications Services 1986, 70).

Uncle Cam and Wycliffe Bible Translators have helped make the church fully aware of the 200 million people who do not have even a single book of the Bible available in their language. A total of 3,200 languages have never been written down, nor are there any linguists studying them. Other organizations have been formed to assist in meeting this glaring need. Dr. Morris Watkins, founder of Lutheran Bible Translators, analyzes the proportions of the task:

> At least 6,400 more linguists are needed—two for each of the 3,200 unwritten languages. But, especially in the larger people groups, it would be much better if there were at least three teams of workers—one team to concentrate on language analysis and translation, one team to concentrate on preparing literacy materials and teaching people to read and train national writers, and another team to concentrate on evangelism and church planting and training the ministry. . . .
>
> In addition to the teams that are working directly with a particular people group, many supportive workers are needed. Airplane pilots are needed to carry teams to remote jungle and mountain villages. Airplane and auto mechanics, teachers for the missionaries' children, buyers, bookkeepers, builders, printers, graphic artists, and many others . . . . At least 12,000 workers are needed to give the Scriptures to these 3,200 people groups, train good leadership, and plant vibrant Christian churches among them. PRAY THE LORD OF THE HARVEST TO SEND FORTH LABORERS INTO HIS HARVEST (Watkins 1987c, 90)!

Townsend, Watkins, and others have helped keep before the church the needs of those who do not have the saving Word of the heavenly Father available in their mother tongue.

Another man of vision who has contributed to the strategy of modern evangelization is Dr. Ralph Winter, director of the United States Center for World Missions (USCWM) in Pasadena, California. "As an initiator, he is without a peer. He has started more missionary agencies than any other living person; all of them are viable operations today"(Kane 1986, 12). Researchers at the USCWM have helped identify 16,000 unreached people groups in the world. One of Winter's most helpful concepts is his identification of four kinds of evangelism. Witnessing to Christians whose faith has grown cold and stands in need of revival he labels as E-0.

> E-1 is sharing the Gospel with a person from your own cultural unit, someone of your own ethno-linguistic group. E-2 is evangelizing a neighboring people or group with a related language. E-3 is reaching out to someone of a totally different language and culture. . . . Evangelism is more challenging and requires greater sensitivity and skill as one moves from E-0 to E-3. Winter's contention is that the world's greatest need at this point in history is a massive increase in E-2 and E-3 evangelism (Rudnick 1984, 218).

The information and publications coming out of Winter's USCWM are but one part of a larger movement: the coming of age of missiology. Missiology is the science of missions. Under its umbrella are disciplines such as mission theology, mission history, methods, strategy, anthropology, intercultural studies, and cross-cultural communication. Although the term may not have been used before the nineteenth century, missiology has always been with us. The difference today is that our information about how to "teach all nations" is multiplying. During the year 1900 only 300 books or articles on evangelization were produced in the entire world. During 1988, approximately ten thousand such titles were produced, involving about 70 major languages. In 1988, 35.5 million computers were in use by Christian churches and agencies. That statistic is estimated to increase nearly tenfold to 340 million by the turn of the century (Barrett 1988, 16-17). This means that computer-wise missionaries and missiologists all over the world are gathering data which will help the church plan its strategy for the final assaults of global Christian outreach.

Missiology is also expanding in seminaries. In the past a single missions professor seemed to be sufficient. Today, some seminaries have an entire school of world mission with several faculty members. Thank the Lord, Lutheran seminaries in North America appear headed in the same direction. All this gathering and disbursing of missiological information does not mean that the kingdom of God will arrive without the power of the Holy Spirit. The power of God is always primary, but missiology will help Christians to announce Christ's kingdom to more people more effectively than ever before.

The Final Assaults (1990 to the Return of Christ)

In this brief sketch of mission history we have rejoiced in the many heroes and successes of the past. Now we come to the most important chapter—the one that will be written by you and me. What will future generations say of our dedication to the global cause that Christ has given to us, His people?

We live in a world in which 2.6 billion people need cross-cultural missionaries to reach out to them. This great challenge is escalated by the population explosion. In the days of Christ, world population was about 200 million. In 1500 it had doubled to about 400 million. In 1830 the population reached one billion. It doubled to two billion by 1930. In July 1986 we could say, "Now we are five billion."

> Although some 130,000 people die every day, about 330,000 babies are born every day. So there is an increase in population of about 200,000 every day, or 73 million per year. At the present annual growth rate of 2%, there will be 6.2 billion people in the world by the year 2000 (Watkins 1987c, 199).

The statistics are mind-boggling. The world grows by a Chicago every month. It grows by a California every four months. Some people may greet these figures with flagging fatalism: "It's hopeless to think we can ever keep up with that growth."

Rather than view the population explosion as a hindrance, however, we ought to greet it as a golden opportunity. Think of it in this light: In the very epoch when God is placing the most souls on earth, He is also providing His church with the strategies and resources to reach those billions of souls with the gospel. Now is not the time to throw up our hands in defeat, simply because the job is big. Now is the time to offer our hands for the task God has set before His mighty army.

There is another reason why our zeal need not falter. For the final assaults, God is providing millions of reinforcements: the new Christians throughout the Two-Thirds World. (The nations that are not aligned with the capitalist or communist superpowers have been commonly called the Third World. However, it is more accurate to call them the Two-Thirds World, because they comprise over two-thirds of the world's population.) By the end of this century, 60 percent of all Christians will be found in the Two-Thirds World. Therefore, obeying the Great Commission is not just up to North American Christians or those from the Western world.

> Being of the same body, there is no essential difference, either in position or responsibility, between the older and younger churches before God. Together they are *the church* through which God speaks in the world. . . . [T]he magnitude of the task of evangelism demands all available personnel, and personal differences must disappear in the work that is shared by Christians of every race and nation (Syrdal 1967, 167).

Mission work was once considered the "white man's burden." Today that concept is being replaced by worldwide Christian teamwork. In 1986, only 13 percent of the world's Protestant missionaries were non-Westerners, but the non-Western missionary force was increasing five times as fast as its Western counterpart. For example, the Evangelical Lutheran Church of Brazil has missionaries in Portugal, Paraguay, and Venezuela; the Japan Evangelical Lutheran Church sends missionaries to reach the large Japanese element in Brazil.

Two-Thirds World missionaries are not short on courage. From the Evangelical Lutheran Church of Papua New Guinea, which has 450 missionaries, comes this tale:

> Another evangelist lived among a tribe that was ceaselessly at war with its neighbors. The evangelist did everything that he could to bring about peace. But each time that he thought he had accomplished his aim, the tribe went off to war again—there was always some score in the blood-feud not yet paid off. At last the evangelist called the men of the tribe together and told them that, if they were convinced that the blood-feud was still crying for a victim, they should kill him [the evangelist]. But, that once done, they should keep the peace. Naturally this offer was not accepted. But the men saw that the evangelist really meant what he said. They caught a glimpse of the love of God, who wanted to give them peace; and so they gave up fighting (Vicedom 1961, 40-1).

Neither do Two-Thirds World mission supporters lack dedication and sacrificial giving. The Friends Missionary Prayer Band of South India, which numbers eight thousand members, supports eighty full-time missionaries in North India. Though they live in poverty, they support one missionary for every hundred members. What an example to us (Winter 1978, 41)!

We expect the Two-Thirds World mission force to increase. God only knows what resources He may raise up.

> If the rapidly growing church in China ever regains full religious freedom and is permitted to send and support missionaries overseas, China, in the twenty-first century, may provide the lion's share of Christian missionaries. Their Asian background, their ability to adapt to other cultures and learn other languages, their ability to endure hardship ("eat bitterness," as they call it), and their reputation for integrity, frugality, and hard work will stand them in good stead when they go out to win the world for Christ (Kane 1986, 38).

The presence of the Two-Thirds World mission force should not lead us to lethargy. Western Christians could excuse themselves from mission work, saying, "We have carried the ball long enough. Now it is their turn." Christ did not tell us to take turns. He commanded all who love His name to take the Gospel everywhere and thus turn the world upside down. Ralph Winter summarizes the matter: "We have potentially a world-wide network of churches that can be aroused to their central mission. . . . No generation has less excuse than ours if we do not do as He asks" (Winter 1981, 176).

The Celebration for All Eternity

We are part of a chain of witnesses that extends through the centuries until Christ our Lord returns in victory. We refer to Christ's final coming as the end of the world, when actually it is merely the end of the beginning, to be followed by eternal life and incomparable joy in the presence of God. Our future in the new heaven and new earth will be a bright and glorious history, for all the citizens will have washed their robes in the blood of the Lamb. As holy, perfect men and women we shall live in a world without hunger or poverty or oppression or prejudice or injustice. "They will neither harm nor destroy on all my holy mountain, for the earth will be full of the knowledge of the Lord as the waters cover the sea" (Is. 11:9).

Where shall the citizens of heaven hail from? The apostle John tells us: "After this I looked and there before me was a great multitude that no one could count, from every nation, tribe, people and language, standing before the throne and in front of the Lamb" (Rev. 7:9). Heaven is going to be multi-ethnic, multi-cultural. What joy there shall be as we praise the Triune God, all proclaiming His mighty deeds in their own tongue, adding to the hymns their own distinctive rhythms and harmonies.

> From earth's wide bounds, from ocean's farthest coast,
> Through gates of pearl streams in the countless host,
> Singing to Father, Son, and Holy Ghost:
> Alleluia! Alleluia!
>
> *Lutheran Worship*, 191, 8

To what may we compare the ecstasy of heaven? We glimpse an example in the emotions felt by the Northern armies at the end of the Civil War. On a breezeless May evening, the Army of the Potomac was camped outside of Washington, D.C. Now, on the eve of their release from military service, they felt listless and at loose ends. You know the feeling. You have felt it at high school graduation or when moving away from a place you have loved. A mother knows that emotion after giving birth to a child. There is a great sense of accomplishment fused to a great sense of loss. Joy and sorrow are all knotted up inside the heart.

> On some impulse a few soldiers got out candles, stuck them in the muzzles of their muskets, lighted them, and began to march down a company street; in the windless twilight the moving flames hardly so much as flickered.
>
> Other soldiers saw, liked the looks of it, got out their own candles, and joined in the parade, until presently the whole camp was astir. Privates were appointed temporary lieutenants, captains, and colonels; whole regiments began to form, spur-of-the-moment brigadiers were commissioned, bands turned out to make music—and by the time full darkness had come, the whole army corps was on the parade ground, swinging in and out, nothing visible but thousands upon thousands of candle flames (Catton 1961, 494).

Then they began to cheer and cheer and cheer! They had marched to a hundred battlefields together. Now they simply marched for the joy of it, and they cheered because their fighting had not been in vain. The Union had been preserved. The slaves had been freed.

The celebration in heaven will be something like that, because Isaiah prophesied, "You have enlarged the nation and increased their joy; they will rejoice before you . . . , as men rejoice when dividing the plunder" (Is. 9:3). The celestial celebration will be far superior to that of the Army of the Potomac for two reasons. First, the soldiers lost most of their camaraderie the very next day, as they became civilians again, parted ways, and returned home to begin the long hard challenge of rebuilding the broken nation. Not so for us! We will all be there together, living in perfect harmony with peoples from all nations. Working side by side and heart to heart, we shall develop the new heaven and the new earth to the glory of God our Creator and Savior.

Secondly, the soldiers had lost their "Captain, O Captain," as Walt Whitman mournfully depicted the fallen Abraham Lincoln. The splintered nation would slowly be reconstructed without the counsel and strength of the president who had called for "malice towards none and charity for all." Not so for us. We shall have our Captain. He is not dead; He is risen! From every land, we shall have come to Mount Zion; to the heavenly Jerusalem, the city of the living God; to multitudes of angels in joyous assembly; to the church of the firstborn, whose names are written in heaven; to God, the judge of all men, to the spirits of righteous men made perfect; to Jesus the mediator of a new covenant through His sprinkled blood (Heb. 12:22-24). We shall know Him more intimately than ever before, for we shall see Him as He is (1 John 3:2).

Eternal life with the loving, saving God—this is the goal toward which world Christians strive. This is why we seek first the kingdom of God and His righteousness. This is why we join ranks with the mighty army of witnesses of past eras, marching from victory on to victory till every foe is vanquished and Christ is Lord indeed. This is the cause for which missionaries sacrifice in order to bring some to Christ. This is the reason that the redeemed witness, pray, and offer their resources to spread the Gospel. This is why we fight the good fight. Because history has a goal, our lives have a glorious purpose.

Eternal life is the exclamation point that joyously punctuates the end of mission history!

Do Something Now

1. *Search Scripture.* Read Acts 17:1-9 to learn how Paul, Silas, and Timothy established a group of believers in Thessalonica. Then read the short letter of 1 Thessalonians, imagining that you are one of the new Christians who first received the letter. Circle the words and phrases that show how missionaries Paul, Silas, and Timothy feel toward you. Underline the words that show how they went about preaching the Word of God.

2. *Read.* For an in-depth view of early Christian witnessing, read *Evan-*

gelism in the Early Church by Michael Green. A thorough coverage of mission history is given in *Speaking the Gospel through the Ages: A History of Evangelism* by Milton L. Rudnick. For popularly written historical sketches of about one hundred missionaries, try *From Jerusalem to Irian Jaya: A Biographical History of Christian Missions* by Ruth A. Tucker.

3. *Listen* to the tape series *The Kingdom Strikes Back!* In a series of lectures given at Bethany Lutheran Seminary, Minneapolis, Dr. Ralph Winter expertly summarizes God's love for unreached peoples down through the centuries. Here is a briefer listening activity. Obtain a copy of the song "Adam, Where Are You?" by Don Francisco. The best way to experience this song is to play it on a tape deck while driving through the city or town where you live. As you drive, look at the people, and imagine how God is calling out to each of them.

4. *Look.* Patrick Johnstone has prepared 32 overhead projector transparencies with maps and graphs. They provide an overview of today's world, the gospel advances, and the unfinished task. Share these colorful visuals with others.

5. *Converse.* Chat with someone whose family has been Christian for at least two generations. Ask him if he knows how his people came to know Christ. Encourage him to investigate who it was that brought his ancestors to Christ and to thank the Lord for sending them that Christian witness.

6. *Pray.* In order to pray intelligently, keep abreast of present mission history as it is being made. *The Harvesters* is a quarterly magazine available free from the Lutheran Church—Missouri Synod. *World Encounter*, a quarterly of the Evangelical Lutheran Church in America, costs $6 per year. For semi-monthly updates on general evangelical missions and world developments, subscribe to *World Pulse,* a publication of the Evangelical Missions Information Service.

Chapter 5
Facets of the Mission Jewel

Just as a jeweler scrutinizes a multi-faceted diamond, so Christians can apply themselves to the study of the vast and varied subject of worldwide Christian outreach. Every ethnic group, every city, every non-Christian religion is another facet in the jewel. There are so many facets that no one but God knows all about cross-cultural ministry. In this chapter we shall discuss four key factors of mission work: (1) the cross-cultural opportunities in North America; (2) the rising importance of urban missions; (3) holistic ministry; and (4) spiritual warfare. As we study these facets, we will find that the mission jewel is a "joy-el," for, as always, the Lord will grant us great joy in serving Him cross-culturally at the end of the 20th century.

Facet 1: North American Opportunities

Believers have tended to separate the church's outreach into two categories. First, we use terms like *evangelism* and *home missions* to mean local witnessing. Second, we often define *foreign missions* or *overseas missions* as outreach that is distant and cross-cultural. This section will demonstrate that it is no longer possible to make such distinctions, because cross-cultural opportunities are all around us. "The mission of the church is as near as the man next door and as inclusive as the whole wide world" (Sease and Voehringer 1963, 5). When you picked up this book, you may have wondered what it had to do with your daily life. After all, mission work is far away, right? Wrong. God is internationalizing His world. He is bringing the world to your door. The issue is whether you will grasp the opportunities He provides. Let us briefly consider some of them.

1. Refugees

Lutherans and other denominations transplanted from Europe have a long history of ministry to immigrants. To newcomers we offered physical assistance and gathered them into congregations so that there would be ongoing spiritual care and growth in Christ. Ample opportunities exist today to carry on this work. The difference is that the present new arrivals are not from "the homeland" and usually do not speak our language. In spite of these difficulties, organizations such as Lutheran Immigration and Refugee Service have helped many congregations welcome thousands of refugees to our shores.

Some church members may object to the influx of immigrants to North America, complaining about loss of jobs and over-population; but compared to some countries, we have nothing to complain about. "The small, less-developed country of Pakistan took in more refugees during 1978 and 1979 than the United States has since 1945" (Wilson and Aeschliman n.d., 88).

In one congregation, the pastor twice confronted the church council with the dire need for churches to sponsor refugees. Both times the response was "We are a small church with only 160 members. We don't have the resources to take on such a project."

Six months later, the pastor voiced the same appeal, but he added, "Before you tell me again, 'It's impossible,' I want you to investigate the matter and prove to me that we can't do it. If your argument is convincing, I won't bring it up again."

They studied, and, lo and behold, they discovered that they might have the resources to handle a family of four. Even when God sent them a family of eleven Laotians, they did not flinch, but grasped the task at hand; and thus they experienced the joy of sharing Christ cross-culturally. What rejoicing there was the day all eleven were baptized! What double joy a year later when six more Laotians turned from Buddhism and received "the washing of rebirth and renewal by the Holy Spirit" (Titus 3:5).

For more information, contact Lutheran Immigration and Refugee Service.

2. Ethnic Groups

Often white middle-class churches have overlooked the opportunity to reach out to ethnic groups, even when they are nearby. For example, there are Lutheran churches planted in the midst of Italian or Polish neighborhoods, and rarely do any of the Lutherans seek to communicate the Gospel to the Italians or Poles. Often it is assumed that, because they are Italian, they must all be Roman Catholics. But that is as foolish as assuming that every person from a Lutheran background is a real Lutheran. Both are false assumptions.

Some ethnic groups in need of the Gospel have been on our continent for generations. There are 1.5 million American Indians in the U. S., and 92 percent do not attend church (Going 1986, 7). Canada is the home of about 1.4 million Amerindians. It would be naive to assume that they all live on reservations. For instance, "there are approximately 20,000 Native Americans in the Twin Cities. Even though a high percentage is baptized as Christians, only 250 attend Sunday worship on a regular basis" ("Urban Indian Ministry" 1986, 3). Certainly a great deal needs to be done to reach these people. Praise God for those who are already working among American Indians. Pray the Lord of the harvest to send more laborers into this field.

Also often overlooked are the Jews, though North America is the home of one-third of all the Jews in the world. Some Christians assume that there is no need to proselytize Jews, because, as "God's chosen people," He must have some special plan for them. He does. It is Jesus Christ, the chosen Savior of both Jews and Gentiles. "Salvation is found in no one else, for there is no other name under heaven given to men by which we must be saved" (Acts 4:12). The Jews for Jesus organization provides a wealth of information about outreach to Jews. The Board for Evangelism Services of the LCMS has developed some excellent materials to help Christians understand Jews and witness to them about their Messiah. *Speak Tenderly to Jerusalem* by C. M. Hanson is another insightful resource.

Yes, we need to be concerned about the evangelization of the ethnic groups that have been among us for years. But in addition, God is bringing many new nations to North America.

> Between 1971 and 1981 India was the third leading source of immigrants to Canada. . . . 60–70,000 Indians live in the Vancouver area. Some cities are 30% East Indian. . . . Twenty cities in B.C. have Sikh temples. . . . 15% of the 2500 residents of Lac la Biche, Alberta, are Muslim. Over 76,000 Muslims live in Alberta and B.C. (Faasch 1988, 3).

The flow of foreigners to our shores is not expected to diminish. The Japanese firms establishing businesses here provide us with new opportunities to give a firm Christian witness. "North America's Chinese population is expected to double by the year 2000 after China's taking control of Hong Kong in 1997 and Macao in 1999" ("Mission Updates: China" 1988, 1). This development would give North America the largest concentration of Chinese outside of Asia.

We could call the mixing of the peoples of the earth "internationalization." The process is not only occurring here but also around the world, especially in urban centers. The influx of peoples is accompanied by an influx of religions with which most Christians are unfamiliar: Hinduism, Buddhism, and Islam.

> We learned about them through missionary reports and college world-religions classes; we observed shadowy imitations of their practices through Hare Krishna gurus, imported meditation techniques, and black professional athletes changing their names to Ali and Abdul.
>
> But now we are faced with these religions in their pure forms. . . . Orthodox Hindus, Buddhists, and Muslims now live in our neighborhoods, send their children to school with our children, and vote in our elections. And their numbers, along with their influence, are growing (Muck 1988, 15).

What does internationalization signify to the average Christian? It does not mean that we should turn tail and hide from the heathen who now live next door. It means that cross-cultural ministry need not be a spectator sport. You can be a missionary right where you are. God in His grace and wisdom is bringing millions of unbelievers nearby so that through our witness they may "seek the Lord while he may be found; call on him while he is near. . . . , for he will freely pardon" (Is. 55:6-7).

3. Hispanics

One ethnic group in particular is so numerous and widespread that it seems to be shouting for the attention of the white middle-class church. Rev. Douglas Groll, Director of the Hispanic Institute of Theology of the LCMS, cites the monumental rise of the Hispanic subculture:

> There are 23 million Hispanics presently in the United States. This country has the fifth largest Spanish-speaking population in the world. It is estimated that by the year 2000, the United States will be the second largest Spanish-speaking country in the world. Some predict there will be over 40 million. The Hispanic population in this nation grew by 65 percent between 1970 and 1980. Hispanics will surpass blacks as the largest minority living in the United States by 1990 ("Hispanic Institute Growing" 1988, 3).

How shall we respond to the growing number of Hispanics in America? Some would like to turn back the clock and ignore this development, but we will do well to learn from the example of a young woman named Priscilla Mundfrom who tells her own story:

> When I was a sophomore in high school, my family moved from Grafton, N.Dak., to Nogales, Ariz.
>
> At the time, I was very confused as to why God would ask me to go to a place that seemed so remote and far from everything and everyone that I knew. My heart was full of questions and anxiety as I moved into a community where the people spoke a different language, practiced different customs, and where I was the minority.
>
> However, as I allowed myself to become involved in this new culture, my eyes and heart were opened to a very warm, friendly and beautiful people. God began to work within me then, although I did not fully realize it, a burden and a love for the Mexican people that has deepened and developed over the years. As I matured in Him, I grew more keenly aware of the needs of this group of people and gained a great desire to work with and among them. . . .
>
> For many Christians, the thought of serving the Lord in a foreign country among people who have different customs and habits is terrifying and beyond their comprehension. But I believe that God has put within my heart a great fascination and eagerness to be involved with people of other cultures. I would rather go and serve the Lord among a people from a different culture than stay here among my own people. I long to see people who have never heard of Jesus hear of His name and the grace He offers and to watch them freely receive His love (Mundfrom 1985, 12-13).

The Lutheran Church-Missouri Synod has designed a bumper sticker which announces: "Lutherans Care." With our words and loving actions may we and other Christians demonstrate to the world at our doors that we do indeed care.

> We care about the millions upon millions of Asians and Hispanics and Middle Easterners and Europeans and American Indians and Caribbeans who have come to a land of freedom and opportunity. We care about the Mexican

working in the restaurant in Minneapolis. We care about the Greek in the butcher shop in New York. We care about the Romanian sewing dresses in Chicago. We care about the Japanese wholesaling stereo equipment in Los Angeles. We care about the Arab pumping gasoline in Detroit. Why do we care? Because God cares (Wagner 1986, 59).

4. Blacks

Perhaps there is no North American cultural gap more difficult to bridge than that between whites and blacks. Attempts have been made to negate the cliché that Sunday morning is the most segregated hour of the week, but much more needs to be done. Rev. Richard Dickinson, a black Lutheran clergyman, expresses this fact with great force:

> The priceless treasures and riches of God's grace in Christ Jesus our Savior are the roses which the Lord has entrusted to the Lutheran Church. . . .
>
> The thorns appear when Black people strive to partake of these precious jewels of salvation, these priceless riches of God in Christ Jesus. If one views the Lutheran Church as a ship carrying this precious cargo and the world as the raging sea, the picture becomes clearer when Blacks are seen as the unsaved, in the water and pleading for help. Lifelines are thrown overboard, but they are rose vines with many thorns. Some persons, with guilty consciences, perhaps, throw some lifeboats overboard, and many Blacks climb into them. . . .
>
> The people on the ship sing cheerful songs to the people who are in the lifeboats and hanging on the lifelines. They also pass down to them choice portions of the riches on board, but they will not lend a hand to help them on board. If they want to come aboard, they must climb the vines, striving to avoid the dangerous and deadly thorns (Dickinson 1977, 11-12).

Is this illustration an overstatement? There are too many cases which prove its truthfulness. Many white congregations in changing neighborhoods have dragged their feet in reaching out to blacks, for fear that the whites would leave. In the end, most of them fled anyhow, leaving a once thriving congregation decimated and ill-equipped to minister in its changed community.

A white Lutheran missionary serving in Africa reports:

> No one will openly admit it, but racism is alive and well in our denomination. A pastor in a changing community once boasted to me that there were none of "them" in his church. When I speak at churches, this statement always gets me, "Have much trouble with the Blacks over there?" Many, many people have expressed how glad they are that we are helping the Blacks "over there"; just don't bring any back here. Until we batter down this racial wall, we as a church are not going to make much progress in evangelizing the world.

This warning should be taken to heart. As long as indifference and prejudice rule our outreach to blacks in our own communities, we will be severely hampered in proclaiming Christ to other peoples around the world.

Lutherans have tended to underestimate their church's appeal to blacks, assuming that they are only interested in other denominations. But Lutherans have much to offer blacks. We have the power of properly proclaiming Law and Gospel. We have the largest Protestant school system on the continent, and church analyst Lyle Schaller observes that private schools are being sought by two-parent, upwardly-mobile black families. Appreciating the benefits of a quality education, they are willing to make the necessary sacrifices. No Protestant denomination is better equipped to meet this need than the Lutheran Church. The question is whether we will fully utilize the black interest in quality education to teach black children and parents about the Savior.

Opening school and church doors to blacks brings many benefits and joy. Immanuel Lutheran in Hillside, Il, just west of Chicago, opened its doors and was blessed by God. In 1987, Pastor Robert Nordlie, in planning the funeral for Henry Blackmon, a black elder of the church, agreed to include the black funeral custom of having a sharing time for family and friends to say a few words. They talked about Henry's vibrant faith in Christ and of their own confidence in the resurrection. This "custom" was so well received that it became a new tradition at an old German Lutheran church. If whites are willing to love blacks, there is a great deal they can teach them about being in God's mission. Amen!

5. Short-term Visitors

Thus far we have mentioned people who, though hailing from all over the world, now call this continent their home. Many others are just visiting, some for a period of days, others for a few years. Regardless of the period of time, our responsibility as good hosts is to provide our guests the opportunity to hear the good news in a meaningful way. It is the only hospitable thing to do.

INTERNATIONAL STUDENTS

Approximately 350,000 international students who come to our university campuses every year make up one group of guests. Many of them come from nations that have officially closed the door to foreign mission work.

> It should be ten times easier to convert a Muslim in America, where he is surrounded by every kind of Christian influence, than to convert the same Muslim . . . in the midst of his own family and under the weight of the age-long traditions of a non-Christian faith (Neill 1970, 97).

They may never again have such an opportunity to hear of Christ. Significantly, these bright and influential men and women will be the future leaders of the world. God only knows what they will accomplish for the Savior when they return home. By the Spirit's power, they could make many wise to salvation. With diplomatic power, they could influence decisions in favor of opening doors for missionaries to enter their land.

If there is a campus nearby, you can carry out a ministry of befriending international students. It does not matter how few there are. One or two will be enough to keep you occupied and to give you a whole new perspective on missions. "But will they be interested in befriending me?" you might wonder. There is little need to worry about that.

> The foreign students in this country are interested in nearly everything we have to offer; they especially appreciate the privilege of visiting in our homes. After all, that is where they will see family life. Besides, they are accustomed to practicing hospitality back home and they miss it severely when they come here. To be invited to spend a weekend in one of our homes is something they will cherish. Even a Sunday dinner is a welcome diversion.
>
> Probably the most difficult time for foreign students is vacation time. In some schools no provision is made for students who remain in the dormitories over the Christmas break. During those weeks students must fend for themselves, . . . Quite often the dining room is closed. Sometimes even the dorms are closed. (Kane 1986, 177).

One Lutheran family makes a practice of inviting Middle Eastern Muslims to their home on Christmas Eve. They, and other Christians who have gathered, read Scriptures and sing carols and hymns for the Muslims, explaining that Christmas is more than Santa Claus and Frosty the Snowman of North American secular mythology. In particular the Christians lay stress on the story of the wise men from the East, from the region of the Muslim guests, who came to worship the Savior of the world. What a Christmas celebration there is when one of the students confesses faith in Christ! After all, Jesus is the reason for the season for international students too.

For added information, check out the June 1988 issue of *Inter-Connections*, a campus ministry publication edited by Hubert Beck, Robert Lange, and Edward Schmidt. Or view the film *The Stranger in Our Midst*, which is available from the LCMS.

SEAMEN'S MINISTRIES

Anyone who lives in or near a shipping port can get involved in an exciting worldwide ministry to seafarers. There are 9 million seafarers, including fishermen, in the world today. Of this number over two-thirds are from countries with limited Christian presence. These men are highly paid, but the work is taxing with no strong union to protect them. They must leave their families for many months at a time, and every port presents a strange new transportation and money system. Only when they finally return home for a brief period are they men with a country.

Just as Jesus, walking by the Sea of Galilee, called fishermen to become disciples, so today there are Christians involved in calling seafarers to follow the Pilot who can guide them to the haven of heaven. During the one to five days that a ship is in port, Christian Seamen's Centers help crew members with many physical, emotional, and spiritual needs. The physical needs may include home cooking, a ride to a shopping center to buy clothes, and a visit to the doctor or dentist. Emotional needs are met by friendliness and a cheery seamen's center equipped with homey furniture, a piano, and a table tennis table. A small quiet room with a telephone is a godsend for men who have not conversed with their loved ones in months.

Spiritual needs are not overlooked. Everyone involved makes it clear that all this love is being expressed because Christ first loved us. Here is an example of how seamen's ministry has touched lives:

> "I'd give my life!" So said a deck officer from India as the "INTER-MARINE VENTURE" was making ready for sea. She had been loading logs at Tacoma. An intelligent man, who had meditated much on the meaning—or apparent meaninglessness—of life, had invited both Chaplain Eckhoff and myself to a restaurant meal.
>
> And it soon became obvious why. With all his Hindu background, he had that deep unfulfilled longing in his heart! "How can I establish communication with God? Or, if you will, how can I find him? . . . and be sure!" So tremendous was his need, that he said quite sincerely he'd give his life if only he could attain his wish.
>
> How wonderful to be able to share with him: "You don't have to give *your* life to get through to God. He's already given *His Son's* to get through to you!" We were able to show him through scripture that his seeking was worked by Him who first sought him. And so, after a time of prayer together, another Hindu came to Christ, unburdened himself at the foot of the Cross, and went his way with new-found joy in his heart . . . and a New Testament and Bible study course in his hand. Pray for him, that he may mature in the faith, share it with his shipmates, and with his wife and three sons back in Bangalore (Kverndal 1979, 1).

The final phrases refer to the Ministering Seafarers Program, a highly effective follow-up system devised by Lutherans that is now used all over the world. Here is how it works: A seafarer whom the Holy Spirit has led to faith is encouraged to be a missionary among his crew mates, who are often a mixture of nationalities. Bible correspondence courses and audio-visual materials are provided for him to share with his mates. The result is that seamen are equipped to share the good news with others. The Ministering Seafarer Program is now standard operating procedure of the International Coordinating Committee for Maritime Follow-up Ministry, an interdenominational network of seamen's ministries in over a hundred port cities of the world. With the aid of computers they coordinate their efforts and provide crew members consistent spiritual care as they voyage from port to port.

If you like to sail, or if you have served in the navy, or if you have always dreamed of adventure on the high seas, perhaps this ministry is for you. For more information, write to the Lutheran Association for Maritime Ministry and subscribe to the newsletter *Mooring Lines*.

These are just some of the cross-cultural mission opportunities which do not require you to board a jet for the other side of the world. You and your congregation do not have to settle for merely hearing the adventures of missionaries working "way over there." You can have your own adventures sharing Christ with the nations which the Lord has placed as near as your own zip code.

Start investigating the possibilities by studying the ethnic make-up of your community. Visit some ethnic churches. Plan a mission education session for your church council. Sponsor a mission festival that includes a neighborhood accent. Begin a vacation Bible school or some other outreach ministry directed at a cultural group you have targeted. For in-depth information, consult Earl Parvin's book *Missions USA*.

Facet 2: The Urban Mission Challenge

Upon hearing the word "missionary," a North American Christian often pictures a man dressed in khaki and a pith helmet, cutting through the jungle with his machete to preach to half-naked savages who humbly address him as *bwana*.

Is this mental image of the typical missionary accurate? Although bush work is still being carried out among many unreached tribes, the lion's share of mission work today must be carried out in modern urban settings. The reason is simple:

> The world is coming to the city. Today, people from each of Mainland China's 31 provinces live in one four block square area of New York City. In 1900, only one person in 40 dwelt in cities; by 1980, the figure was one out of three.
>
> By the year 2000, 94 percent of the people of North America, 78 percent of Europeans, 76 percent of Latin Americans, 42 percent of Asians and 45 percent of Africans will live in urban areas.
>
> Today there are 290 cities in the world with more than one million inhabitants. By the year 2000, there will be at least 500 cities in this category. Mexico City will have a projected population of 31 million; Sao Paulo, 26 million; Tokyo-Yokohama, 24 million; and Shanghai, 23 million ("Should I Not Be Concerned about That Great City?" *Harvesters* 1987, 1).

Even though urban centers must be the primary targets of future evangelistic outreach, many North American Christians assume that ministry in modern cities does not merit the title "mission work." More than once the following conversation has occurred between a furloughing missionary and a North American churchgoer:

Layman: Why are you wasting your time in that city?
Missionary: Why do you say that, sir?
Layman: I was there once on a trip. It's a modern city with traffic jams, skyscrapers, and television. Why waste your time there, when they already have all the advantages of modern technology?

Missionary: Sir, does owning a car or a television make someone a child of God?

Layman: Well, no. Only faith in Christ does that.

Missionary: We do not go overseas to share the "blessings" of modern technology but to share the eternal blessings that come from knowing Christ as one's Savior.

Is the need to share Christ as urgent in cities as in the bush? Lutheran deaconess Carol Lee Halter, serving in the modern city of Hong Kong, warns us not to be fooled by the veneer of civilization:

> I am now looking out the window of my 14th floor apartment, and I see many buildings around mine. I live here in Mei Foo Sun Chuen which, when it was built, was the largest private housing project in the world. In the small area of about 1/2 mile by 1/2 mile, there are 86,000 people. The over 100 buildings are almost exactly alike. Each building is 20 floors high and each floor has 6-8 apartments.
>
> What thoughts go through my mind as I look out the window at the many other twenty-story buildings that surround mine? . . .
>
> The first one is, "God, there are so many people out there, and so few of them know you." It breaks my heart when I look out and see so many apartments where they have incense burning to the idols which cannot help them. . . . If only these people could all know the true God, then they would no longer have to live fearing the demons and trying to appease the gods. Yet only ten percent of the people in Hong Kong know the Lord Jesus Christ—5% Protestant and 5% Catholic. The harvest is plentiful, but the laborers are few.
>
> . . . My second thought is, "Thank you, Lord, that I am here and can have at least a small part in bringing the Gospel of the Lord Jesus Christ to the Chinese people" (Halter 1988, 1-2).

Yes, the cities of the world teem with people for whom Christ died, but the saving Word has not been proclaimed to them all.

Negative Attitudes toward the City

Another obstacle to urban ministry is that North American Christians tend to fear the problems related to urbanization. The city, they believe, is the source of all modern ills: crime, drugs, AIDS, prostitution, and so on. Because of this fear, many middle-class churches have avoided serious, concerted outreach to their own cities. When an overseas missionary arrives emphasizing the need for city ministry, his comments hit too close to home. Folks expect to hear about problems like polygamy and poor agriculture, but mention of urban poverty, poor education, and toxic pollution reminds them of the dilemmas that perplex their own country.

We would much rather hear about ministry in the bush or the jungle, because we wrongly assume that rural life is pristine and godly. Only country folk proudly declare, "This is God's country!" Meanwhile, we assume that the city has become the domain of fallen man.

The city became secularized, and too often the church's way of coping with it was to insulate itself, enabling it to gather in a holy huddle and praise Jesus, singing about the heavenly city while ignoring the one in which they lived. Meanwhile, the mandate has not changed. To hallow him who is in the heavenly city is to pray and work that his will might be done in the cities on earth (O'Brien 1984, 209).

To take world evangelization seriously, we will have to take urban ministry seriously. To take urban ministry seriously, we must be willing to trust God to protect, direct, and equip us as we serve in the city. Herman Gockel states this truth beautifully:

> Looking out over the teeming city [of Los Angeles], our friend observed almost sadly: "As long as you and I live there will never again be a routine day, a routine week, a routine month, a routine year."
>
> How true! The routine days and weeks of yesteryear are gone forever. . . . Our todays can scarcely recognize our yesterdays, and our tomorrows will be hard put to recognize today. And this is true in almost every area of life: in science and technology, in politics and government, in morals and religion. . . .
>
> We have no promise of a routine future. We *do* have the promise of an unchanging and unchangeable Christ. With Him at our side we can leave all yesterdays behind and walk securely into tomorrow—no matter *what* tomorrow holds (Gockel 1968, 124-25).

Urban Ministry Demands New Strategies

Serving in the city will require different approaches from service in rural areas. The Boy Scouts realize this. In Singapore, with a population of 2.6 million, the scouts are urged to give up their traditional "jungle" activities and convert themselves into city scouts by preparing for emergencies such as car crashes, elevator breakdowns, and water rationing (Trexler 1977, 6).

If the Boys Scouts need to make such adjustments, certainly the church of Christ must do the same. The traditional missionary methods developed in the jungle or village will be relatively useless in the cities of the world. New strategies are called for. Churches must retool; and retooling, whether in a factory or a church, is a costly procedure. To reach the cities will cost both time and money, as we experiment with new strategies and take risks to determine what are the most effective means of reaching out to urban people. But we do not have to do everything by trial and error. Church leaders can learn from sister churches around the world that are already carrying on successful urban ministries. For example, in 1987, Prof. Harley Kopitske of Concordia Seminary in St. Louis visited Venezuela.

> Kopitske reported being "most impressed with the urban strategies being developed jointly by the LLL's *Christ For All Nations'* staff and LCMS missionaries. Radio and TV spots, store-front contact centers, correspondence and home Bible classes, team ministries, ministry area coordinators,

leadership training, felt-needs approaches, friendship evangelism, community involvement, theological education by extension (TEE), tentmaking ministries, audio and videocassette materials for youth, telephone Dial-A-Message Christian counseling and education—these comprise only part of an extensive list of strategies/approaches. They can be applied in North American urban mission areas as well as overseas! And must be!'' ("Urban Outreach Strategies'' 1987, 1).

If North American churches will listen and learn from their sister churches around the world, other strategies will no doubt emerge to help us deal with the mission challenges we have next door.

Yet the main thing, of course, is not who has the best methods and strategies. The main thing is proclaiming Christ to those who do not know Him. One such person was Victor Diaz of Caracas, Venezuela. Just a few years ago, Victor's life had fallen apart: his wife had filed for divorce; he was drinking too much; and suicide was beginning to sound like an alluring means of escape. Riding on a bus, he heard a radio announcer ask, "Is your marriage on the rocks?'' Riveted by that question, Victor listened to *A Moment with God*, and a spark of hope began to glimmer. A few weeks later, through the caring witness of several Christians, the Holy Spirit worked a miracle of faith in Victor's heart. For more details about this true story, order from the International Lutheran Laymen's League the film *The Story of Victor*, in which Victor plays himself.

Today Victor is an urban Christian sharing his Savior with urban people who have urban problems. Specifically, Victor is reaching out to drug addicts and convicts, striving to meet both their physical needs and their spiritual needs. This brings us to the next facet of the mission jewel.

Facet 3: Mission Work Is Holistic

Christ our Savior went from town to town, "preaching the good news of the kingdom and healing every disease and sickness'' (Matt. 9:35). In like manner, Christians are called to reach out to the world in the name of Christ by attending to people's physical and spiritual needs. This is called holistic ministry. To seek to remedy only the spiritual needs or only the physical needs would not be holistic, but half-istic.

There are two reasons that we should serve people holistically. First, simply because Jesus told us to love even our enemies, we fulfill the Great Commission—go, make disciples, baptize, and teach—as we obey the Great Commandment—love one another. Secondly, often a physical, economic, or emotional problem makes it difficult for a person to hear and grasp the Gospel. Christians cannot allow the problem to persist; rather they strive to remove the obstacle.

> Because the distress of external circumstances, as well as the evils within, can obstruct the way to God, a faith that is prepared to help must address itself to the whole man in his actual condition and must offer to help

76

with both hands; the Word with the right hand and love with the left. It must bring forgiveness *and* fellowship, the physician *and* the remedy, the bread of life *and* daily bread (Koberle 1964, 199).

The Great Debate

In Christian circles there is a continuing debate over which kind of ministry is more important: spiritual or physical. It can be argued, and rightly so, that proclaiming the bread of life has more lasting, eternal effect than handing out bread to the hungry. Even if we succeeded in lifting all the poor to a higher, healthier standard of living, they would still lack the saving grace of Him who, though He was rich, yet for our sakes became poor, so that we through His poverty might become rich (2 Cor. 8:9). Yet the New Testament reports that social ministry was an essential part of orthodoxy. In Galatians 2 Paul relates how he went to Jerusalem to "set before them the gospel that I preach among the Gentiles" (Gal. 2:2). After hearing Paul and Barnabas out, the elders of the church in Jerusalem gave them the right hand of fellowship and asked only one thing of them: "that we should continue to remember the poor, the very thing I was eager to do" (Gal. 2:10). Paul's ministering to physical needs was considered to be as important as the content of his preaching. "Dear children, let us not love with words or tongue but with actions and in truth" (1 John 3:18).

Which is more important, evangelism or social ministry? Christ's church must affirm both, because God treats us holistically. He not only saves our souls; He also promises us new resurrected bodies. To argue over which ministry we shall emphasize is like debating which wing of an airplane is more important. When your plane is accelerating down the runway about to leave terra firma, wouldn't you prefer to have both wings on the jet? Similarly, our outreach ministries will not fly if we do not have a balanced, holistic approach.

An excellent example of this balance is the work Lutherans have performed among deaf and blind people. They pioneered deaf ministry in North America. Many everyday church members find satisfaction in assembling braille materials for the blind. This work has a definite cross-cultural dimension. Lutheran Braille Workers, Inc. has produced Scriptures and books in many languages. By the Holy Spirit's power, the dots about Jesus are effective. "A girl in Mexico wrote, 'I was born blind and have never seen a face. Now that I know about Jesus, His will be the first face I'll ever see' " (Koehler 1986, 75). Responses like that motivate the braille workers to continue their mission of mercy.

Levels of Christian Social Ministry

When we speak of meeting human needs, we must recognize that there are different levels of assistance that can be offered. Those involved in holistic ministry speak of relief, rehabilitation, development, and justice. It is helpful to think of these terms in a continuum, for they are not strict, airtight divisions but activities that blend from one into the other.

Relief is the immediate aid that is sent in the event of a disaster or tragic circumstances. The Good Samaritan brought relief in an emergency (Luke 10:25-37). Dorcas was a provider of relief to the poor of Joppa (Acts 9:36).

Rehabilitation "may mean enabling people to rebuild their homes after an earthquake or flood, to secure some type of work, or to regain and improve their former state" (Weber 1979, 9). In a sense, God gave ancient Israel a perpetual form of rehabilitation in the gleaning laws, which ordered farmers to leave a small part of their harvest in the fields, to be gleaned by foreigners, orphans, and widows (Deut. 24:19-22; Lev. 19:9-10).

The third level, development, is needed because poor people not only lack money—they lack options. Because of poverty, deficient education, disease, disaster, or political-economic oppression, few if any options are open to them. Development results in one's having more options. The Lord gave the Jewish nation a permanent means of development in the legislation regarding the Year of Jubilee, which is recorded in Lev. 25:8-55. Imagine the feelings of the poor when the Year of Jubilee rolled around and they again gained access to the means of production.

Justice, the fourth level of aid, means being advocates for those having little influence at the centers of economic and political power and "helping to reform laws, systems, structures and institutions in an effort to create more justice" (LCUSA n.d., 3). Such activities bring us into politics and economic theories, a realm in which the middle-class church has avoided involvement. However, we must be willing to strive for justice if we are going to take seriously the Lord's Word in Prov. 24:11-12:

> Rescue those being led away to death; hold back those staggering toward slaughter. If you say, "But we knew nothing about this," does not he who weighs the heart perceive it? Does not he who guards your life know it? Will he not repay each person according to what he has done?

Changes in Attitudes

If we are going to take development and justice issues seriously, we will have to open our eyes wide enough to change some long-held assumptions. Here is one for a starter: Middle-class North Americans are somewhere in the middle between the rich and poor of the world. It isn't so. We are rich.

"No way," you object. "I've got a mortgage, two car payments, and kids in braces. There are piano lessons and college expenses. I seem to go broke every time I bring home a load of groceries. How do all those bills make me rich?"

Remember that *rich* is a relative term. Compared to celebrities and corporation vice presidents, our income might look slim, but compared to most of the poor of our world, we enjoy many benefits of wealth.

> The poorest third of the world's countries have average infant mortality rates of 140 deaths per 1,000 live births. Those who survive infancy can only expect to live to be 47; only 28 percent of the men and 9 percent of the women will ever learn to read. These countries have gross national products (GNP) averaging $320 per person per year.
>
> Looking at the same statistics for the rich third of the world's countries, it's hard to believe they share the same planet. Infant mortality rates are around 12 per 1,000 live births; average life expectancy is 74 years, literacy around 90 percent and GNP $18,405 (Wilson and Aeschliman n.d., 63-64).

Yes, we are rich. Poor people don't worry about mortgages. They consider themselves lucky to have a tin roof over their heads. They don't have car payments; two bare or ill-shod feet supply all the transportation they can afford. Braces? The poor consider themselves lucky if they still have most of their teeth. Piano lessons and college are things they never dream of. And grocery expenses? If a visitor from the Two-Thirds World saw a restaurant with a sign "All You Can Eat," he would shake his head in wonder, mumbling, "I have never had all I can eat at any meal in my whole life" (Nicholson 1984, 82).

The sooner you realize you are rich, the sooner you will realize that you and the blessings God has given you can make significant contributions to alleviate poverty, hunger, and other deficiencies. Also, the better you will understand the Scriptures. Remember all those verses that talk about how the rich should treat the poor? They aren't talking about someone else; they are aimed at you and me.

Now for a pair of assumptions that require reexamination: U. S. foreign policy always has the best interests of others in mind; and capitalism always has positive effects. So that I will not have to take all the objections on this matter, allow me to quote Dr. J. Herbert Kane, a leading Evangelical missiologist who is far from being a left-wing critic. "To some extent," Kane asserts, "the poverty in the Third World is perpetuated by the unscrupulous policies of the powerful multinational corporations based in the West" (Kane 1986, 45). He further states:

> Following the Yom Kippur War in October 1973, the oil-producing countries of the Middle East threatened to cut off their supply of oil to the West. In the ensuing years they raised the price of oil some 400 percent, and we shouted foul play. But that is exactly the kind of game we had been playing for centuries. Our multinational corporations are still driving hard bargains all around the world.
>
> Much of the violence in the Third World today is due more to economics than to politics. The rich are in favor of the status quo. The poor, on the other hand, are determined to overthrow the status quo and establish a government more responsive to their needs. And the bloodshed will continue until some degree of justice is achieved (Kane 1986, 64-65).

Dr. Al Senske, director of LCMS World Relief, adds, "36 of the world's 40 poorest countries export food to the United States" (Senske 1988, 1). Such observations call us to take our role as world citizens more seriously than our role as American or Canadian citizens. The proper priority between these allegiances will appear when we give first place to being citizens of heaven, not striving for our "piece of the pie," but "looking forward to the city with foundations, whose architect and builder is God" (Heb. 11:10).

Rubbing Shoulders with the Unlovely

For holistic ministry to be effective, we cannot just send a check. Someone has to enter the lives of the people trapped in problems and sins.

> A man with leprosy came to him and begged him on his knees, "If you are willing, you can make me clean."
> Filled with compassion, Jesus reached out his hand and touched the man. "I am willing," he said. "Be clean!" Immediately the leprosy left him and he was cured (Mark 1:40-42).

Jesus touched the leper. He affirmed the outcast as a fellow human being. Whom can you and I touch?

Wrestling against the grave social ills of our world will not be easy. Consider, for example, prostitution.

> Prostitutes are sad victims of abuse. They live from day to day, beaten half to death by pimps, treated like cheap lovers, forced into dependency on drugs, exchanged for other prostitutes and even flown to foreign cities and countries to satisfy different customers. . . .
> Prostitution is advanced by the 264 pornographic magazines published around the world, organized sex tours, military bases, topless bars and night clubs. It is big business, making a profit on human lust and the economic desperation of its victims. Most of those caught in the system enter prostitution because it's the only way they can put bread on the table. Young children are often forced into it by parents for this reason. In Paris alone, 8,000 boys and girls under the age of 18 work as prostitutes (Wilson and Aeschliman n.d., 62-63).

Confronted by such a system of evil, is there any hope of snatching some from the slavery of prostitution? Through Christ, yes, as is proven by a true story from the Philippines (Beals 1985, 193-94).

After fourteen years as a prostitute and madam, Aling Maria was burdened with guilt for her sordid life. Through the ministry of a Baptist pastor named Danny Pantoja, Aling Maria learned of the forgiving love and mercy of Jesus Christ. Moved by the Holy Spirit, she trusted in the Savior and became a new creation.

Today Aling Maria and her pastor have a dream of reaching out to other prostitutes. They hope to establish a low-cost restaurant, free of the liquor, lust, and debauchery prevalent in the red light district of Subic Bay. It will be staffed by former prostitutes who have found new life and hope in Christ. Since uniforms are very popular in the Philippiines, these converted women will wear uniforms with a unique embroidered logo—a pile of stones.

Prostitutes seeking food and calm refuge in that restaurant will no doubt ask the waitresses/witnesses, "What is the meaning of those stones?" And the response shall be a heartfelt retelling of the story of the woman caught in adultery, to whom Jesus said, "Neither do I condemn you. . . . Go now and leave your life of sin" (John 8:11). May God bless Aling Maria's dream and make it a reality.

Another group of people that causes fear and trepidation consists of the men and women who sit in prisons around the world. Who will penetrate the concrete and bars of "the slammer" to love them for Christ? Who will penetrate the flint veneer in which these "dregs of society" encase their personalities and souls? Christians can, armed with the Spirit's power and the Spirit's Word of reconciliation with the Father! It doesn't require professionals to do such work. Everyday Christians are often the best.

Usually Christians assume that hardened prostitutes, drug addicts, and criminals are impossible to reach with the Gospel. With that conclusion, we make the same mistake as the Pharisees and teachers of the law who criticized Jesus for mixing with tax collectors and "sinners." The Pharisees assumed that these were the hopeless cases. But, in reality, they are the cases which reveal to us that there is always hope wherever Christians are bold enough to love people and point them to the Savior. Ron Nikkel of Prison Fellowship expresses it this way:

> I came to this job with professional training in criminology, and of course I still try to incorporate everything I learned. But I have gradually become convinced that the lasting answer to prison problems is not rehabilitation, but transformation. Initially, I hesitated to use phrases like "Christ is the answer," but, frankly, I've seen that phrase proved true. I learned certain words in childhood, but the prisoners themselves finally gave meaning to those words. They proved the reality of a theology that had been little more than a mental exercise for me. (Yancey 1988, 20).

There is a real world, full of real and hurting people. With the Holy Spirit's power, you and I can serve them in a holistic manner, bringing them authentic compassion and a Savior who truly died and rose for them.

The Cost of Holistic Ministry

"I know you are right," some readers may respond, "but outreach to those in need just sounds too hard. I don't know how to relate to people like that. In fact, they sort of turn me off. I'm too spoiled and set in my tightfisted and tighthearted ways. And besides, I could not take the emotional toll." Let's deal with those objections one at a time.

1. You don't feel comfortable with some kinds of people. Join the club. Everyone feels that way at the start, but adjusting to people—rather than ignoring them or expecting them to adjust to you—is what serving in another culture or environment is all about. The Holy Spirit has helped many everyday Christians to bridge this gap. He can do the same for you.

2. Do you fear you cannot help the poor and troubled because you are too used to the frills of life? That may be so at the moment, but helping those who have less than you will help you recognize the essentials of life more clearly than ever before. When we serve others with Christlike love, we learn from them lessons we would never gain anywhere else. We will be set free to rearrange our priorities and recognize the trappings of middle-class affluence for what they are—traps.

3. You wonder if you can endure the emotional toll of serving broken people, especially when many of them do not even want to be repaired. I cannot lie; caring ministry will take you to the limit, but it is at the limit that we grow in faith. Muscles are not built up by lifting a ten-pound metal bar. To get rock-hard biceps, you have to put weights on the barbell. For Christians, the weights that transform spiritual flab to tough discipleship are the hard-to-love people and the hard-to-endure ministries that require us to rely solely on God.

A Lutheran friend of mine lifts weights like this every Friday night from 10 p.m. to 2 a.m. Those are the hours Bruno Daube "patrols" the streets and cafes of the Uptown district of Chicago, as a member of the Ecumenical Night Ministry. Uptown does not appear to be a particularly bad neighborhood during the day, but late at night the streets and small restaurants swarm with homeless drifters, runaway kids, drug users and pushers, teenage prostitutes and pimps.

"One bitter January night," Bruno recounts with excitement, "I was walking down a street and noticed a fellow trying to shelter himself on the stoop of a building. A book lay on his knee; it was a Bible. When he saw me, he was startled and, assuming I was the owner of the building, apologized for sitting there. When I told him of a church where he could get a hot meal and a warm bed, he beamed with delight. 'I have been sitting here praying for a place to stay,' he said, 'and God sent you.'

"Do you know how that makes me feel?" Bruno asks rhetorically. "What a privilege it is to be the answer to someone's prayer! So many Christians pray every day for God to bless them. I have learned that the greatest sign of God's presence in one's life is not to receive a blessing but to be one."

This does not mean that Bruno's ministry is easy. Sometimes he feels like giving up. On the first warm evening in March he arrived at his "turf" cheered by the pleasant weather. Then he saw what was blowing in with the balmy breeze—carload after carload of prostitutes with their parasitic pimps. During the winter months their business had been restricted by the cold. As sure a sign of spring as the first robin, the waves of whores washed out on the sidewalk to ply their trade, leaving their clients and themselves emptier than before.

Bruno came home that night despondent. "Lord, what good am I doing here?" he lamented. "What a fool I am to imagine that my few drops of goodness can purify a cesspool of vice."

Two days later, still broken in spirit, Bruno went to the small prayer service held at his church, St. John's Lutheran in Lombard, Illinois. There he shared his frustration and agony. His brothers and sisters in Christ gathered around him, laid their hands on his head and shoulders, and pleaded that God would equip him again for His service. Renewed and revitalized, Bruno—God's answer to prayer—returned to the night ministry.

God is faithful to those who extend themselves to the limits of endurance for the sake of Christ and His Gospel.

> We do not want you to be uninformed, brothers, about the hardships we suffered in the province of Asia. We were under great pressure, far beyond our ability to endure, so that we despaired even of life. Indeed, in our hearts we felt the sentence of death. But this happened that we might not rely on ourselves but on God, who raises the dead. He has delivered us from such a deadly peril, and he will deliver us (2 Cor. 1:8–10).

Facet 4: Mission Work Is Spiritual Warfare

Jesus Christ "went around doing good and healing all who were under the power of the devil, because God was with him" (Acts 10:38). Lutherans are practiced in declaring that the Savior delivers from sin, death, and the power of the devil. This statement has critical implications for world evangelization, because Christ continues to deliver from the power of the devil at the end of the 20th century.

Is the Spirit World Real?

Missionaries to Nigeria Jim and Billy Tyler share information about a rescue that occurred in their ministry:

> Quite a few of our group were going to visit a family of church members whose only son in a family of eight girls had died five days before. . . .
>
> We read Scripture, sang and prayed to console the grieving father. As we were leaving, he blurted out: "I am beyond consolation, my youngest female child is even now dying. We have taken her to the hospital, they could not help. We have tried giving her glucose by mouth; she does not take it. She is now with the mother, in the house of a woman who has knowledge [of witchcraft]. She has not taken food in three days. She is dying."
>
> We saw them outside the door—relatives, friends and neighbors—looking at us with hate and disagreement. We sensed the oppressive presence of Satan. It was frightening. . . .
>
> (We understood that according to tradition, this child's death would be a type of passive sacrifice for the sudden death of the only male child. This was the demand of one of their traditional gods.)
>
> We drove a short distance to a very crowded part of the slum area and parked. We then walked for a while, winding our way back into an inner compound.
>
> We came to the place—a very small dark room with about seven people sitting around. We sat on one of the beds with the mother. . . .

"Did she take any fluids today?"

"No, she won't take."

"Let's take her to the hospital. She must have treatment tonight."

The mother looked to her friends, who indicated "no." We felt heavily burdened and had a strange fear.

It was now late in the evening. We pleaded and finally bargained for the friends to let us, with the parents, take the baby to a hospital.

The heavy darkness we felt was something more than the night. These people could blame us if the cursed child lived, and the parents could be troubled in their faith if she died.

The hospital at first refused us because the doctor was gone for the evening. We begged the nurses to do something to try to save the child's life.

The next day the baby was better. On the second day she was active and eating. We were jubilant!

Alas, on the third day little Seiyefer was taken out of the hospital by her mother and taken back to the house of the lady with "special knowledge."

All right, we said to ourselves, that's it. We have worked, taught and prayed with this family. "Oh, Lord, do you want these non-Christians to continue to mock this man? It is all in Your hands, Lord," we prayed.

God's answer: the little girl lived. Two weeks later, the entire family came to church and asked for time to speak, to give thanks and praise to God that His power is stronger than that of Satan, and His love is wonderful (Tyler 1986, 5).

When missionaries tell tales like this, some North Americans tend to think along these lines: "Oh, those poor, ignorant heathen. They foolishly imagine that witches and spells, ghosts and evil spirits are real." And when foreigners learn that many of us view these things as fables, do you know how they react? "Oh, those poor, ignorant Westerners. They foolishly imagine that witches and spells, ghosts and evil spirits are only figments of our imagination."

So who is right? Westerners tend to assume that all magic, spiritism, and occult practices are nothing more than sham and unfounded superstition. Only uneducated people would believe such myths, we assume. We pride ourselves on being so perceptive. But are people in other lands really that stupid? To assume so is pretentious on our part. In some cases the spell-caster, fortune-teller, or seance medium is nothing more than a charlatan. However, in many cases there are real spirits lurking behind the idols, real power in their spells, real visual effects in their seances, and some degree of accuracy in their fortune-telling. Many missionaries are aware of this reality, but they rarely mention it back home, because they doubt that anyone will take them seriously.

If there is a real power behind some magical and occult practices, whose power is it? The missionary Paul wrote, "Put on the full armor of God so that you can take your stand against the devil's schemes. For our struggle is not against flesh and blood, but against the rulers, against the authorities, against the powers of this dark world and against the spiritual forces of evil in the heavenly realms'' (Eph. 6:11–12). Paul would accept the Tyler story from Africa as an example of warfare against demonic beings that can actually contribute to the death of a child.

Former pagan priests, witch doctors, and mediums who today confess Christ declare that Satan and his minions are the power behind the occult. Fallen angels whisper information to fortune-tellers and clairvoyants. Demons work through spells to influence and harm people. At a seance, evil spirits impersonate the dead, in order to feed people a pack of lies about what happens after death.

You see, unbelievers are not so gullible as we think they are. They do not believe blindly. They have seen evidence of supernatural power, and they often mistakenly conclude that the power comes from divine beings. Meanwhile, Satan cackles with glee, for as long as they believe his lies, they cannot know the truth that will set them free. ''The god of this age [Satan] has blinded the minds of unbelievers, so that they cannot see the light of the gospel of the glory of Christ, who is the image of God'' (2 Cor. 4:4). Satan ''was a murderer from the beginning, not holding to the truth, for there is no truth in him. When he lies, he speaks his native language, for he is a liar and the father of lies'' (John 8:44).

Meanwhile, as North Americans drift farther and farther from Christian truth, Satan is able to work more openly than he did a generation ago. Spiritism and the occult are on the rise. Police files are stuffed with crimes related to satanic worship and human sacrifice. The New Age religions are just 20th century rehashings of the pagan religions that missionaries have dealt with for years. UFO sightings are another satanic charade designed to divert people from knowing the one true God. No longer can we cling to the modern myth that all these things are nothing more than myths.

Mission Possible

Why have I alarmed you with all this talk of Satan's power? For two reasons. First, world evangelization is spiritual warfare. We are not playing a little religious game, hoping that a few people will be persuaded to join our club we call a church. There is a war going on. We Christians are the forces of God who rescue men and women from the dominion of darkness to bring them into the safety of the kingdom of the Son God loves, in whom we have redemption, the forgiveness of sins (Col. 1:13–14). Like Paul, we are sent to open their eyes and turn them from darkness to light and from the power of Satan to God, so that they may receive forgiveness of sins and a place among those who are sanctified by faith in Christ (Acts 26:18).

The second reason is this: We are going to win the war! So let's not be afraid to fight the battles! Often discussion of Satan's wiles and power makes Christians shiver in fear. The devil seems so menacing that we dread meeting him on the battlefield. That is precisely how the enemy wants us to feel, because an army that believes it is outmatched cannot win. During the Civil

War, Robert E. Lee's Confederate forces were always outnumbered. But Lee was a master of deception. He would march the same troops through camp several times in order to convince Union observers that he had a horde of rebels at his command. Because of this military charade, a string of Union commanders, convinced that they were outnumbered two to one, never pressed Lee's forces and lost battle after battle. Finally after three years, Lee met a soldier who was his equal. When Ulysses S. Grant took charge of the Army of the Potomac, he immediately engaged Lee's forces and pressed them incessantly until the war was over. Grant succeeded where so many others had failed because he never doubted that his army was the stronger.

Let's not doubt it either. Our Field Marshall declared, "All authority in heaven and on earth has been given to me" (Matt. 28:18). The Father "seated him at his right hand in the heavenly realms, far above all rule and authority, power and dominion, and every title that can be given, not only in the present age but also in the one to come" (Eph. 1:20–21). Trusting in Christ's unequalled power, you can "put on the full armor of God, so that when the day of evil comes, you may be able to stand your ground, and after you have done everything, to stand" (Eph. 6:13).

Space does not permit me to discuss the details of engaging in spiritual warfare. Of the dozen books that I have read on the subject, the best is *The Adversary* by the Baptist minister Mark Bubeck, available from Moody Press. No other book does such a great job of assuring the reader of the supremacy of God's power over Satan. Lutherans will feel at home with Bubeck's emphasis on the objective truth and reliability of Christian doctrine. *The Adversary* is a manual on how to pray against Satan's power. In fact, a full quarter of the book consists of magnificent Scriptural prayers which illustrate how to use the armor of God to resist the roaring lion and tear down his strongholds by standing firm in the faith (1 Pet. 5:8–9; James 4:7; 2 Cor. 10:4–5).

With bold proclamation and with prayer that rests on the authority of Christ, we can witness victories over Satan such as the one the Lord worked in the life of a woman named Elsa:

> Satan has been working overtime in our newly formed congregation in Caracas. Elsa, one of a number of people that we confirmed last December, became mysteriously ill the same day she was confirmed. If it had not been for the prompt attention given to her by her nephew who is a medical doctor, she would have died that same night. None of the doctors have been able to explain why an otherwse healthy adult woman became so ill so quickly. However, Elsa's relatives believe the reason is because she had been confirmed in the Lutheran Church that day. They claimed that her dead mother's spirit was angry with her and had come back to punish her. It seems that her mother had been an active participant in witchcraft and spiritism. Elsa spent over a month in a cousin's apartment unable to take care of herself. It wasn't until she moved back to her apartment that she realized that her relatives, anticipating her death, had moved all of her belongings out of her apartment and had already attempted to sublet it. It was at that point when we accidentally ran into her, by God's providence, that she told us all that

had happened to her since her confirmation. Because of her relatives' influence she had been led to consult a medium and had begun a process of protection against evil spirits as recommended by the medium. Even though Venezuela is nominally Roman Catholic, such spiritualistic beliefs and practices are extremely common.

Through counseling in the Word of God and encouragement from church members, Elsa has been strengthened and renewed in her faith in Jesus as her Savior from Satan, evil spirits, and eternal death. Since that time, Elsa has brought the good news of Jesus to others and has recently been bringing a friend with her to our worship services. Please pray that God's Word will continue to prevail over the demonic powers and lies which are at work here in Caracas (Selle 1988, 1).

Note that closing request. Through prayer you and I can join in the spiritual battles being fought all around the world. Prayer for missionaries, for local pastors, and for your own witnessing is not reciting a list of "God blesses." It is warfare, calling upon the power of God to win the struggles being fought "against the spiritual forces of evil in the heavenly realms" (Eph. 6:12).

"Is all this Lutheran?" some may ask. Consider the following hymn and then answer the question. Christians involved in ministry to people who are oppressed by demons consider these stanzas one of the best expressions of spiritual warfare ever written. I have used a modern translation so that the text may strike you in a fresh manner.

> A mighty fortress is our God,
> A sword and shield victorious
> He breaks the cruel oppressor's rod
> And wins salvation glorious.
> The old satanic foe
> Has sworn to work us woe.
> With craft and dreadful might
> He arms himself to fight.
> On earth he has no equal.
>
> No strength of ours can match his might.
> We would be lost, rejected.
> But now a champion comes to fight;
> Whom God himself elected.
> You ask who this may be?
> The Lord of hosts is he,
> Christ Jesus, mighty Lord,
> God's only Son, adored.
> He holds the field victorious.
>
> Though hordes of devils fill the land
> All threat'ning to devour us,
> We tremble not, unmoved we stand;
> They cannot overpow'r us.
> Let this world's tyrant rage;

In battle we'll engage.
His might is doomed to fail;
God's judgment must prevail!
One little word subdues him.

God's Word forever shall abide,
No thanks to foes, who fear it;
For God himself fights by our side
With weapons of the Spirit.
Were they to take our house,
Goods, honor, child, or spouse,
Though life be wrenched away,
They cannot win the day.
The Kingdom's ours forever!

Martin Luther

Do Something Now

1. *Search Scripture*. Take a look at Acts 1:8 while referring to a map of the Holy Land in the days of Jesus. In relation to your present address, what places would correspond to Jerusalem, Judea, Samaria, and the ends of the earth? Consider the three "and's" that connect these locations. Do you think Jesus meant them as consecutive targets or simultaneous targets of outreach?

2. *Read*. To gain a richer understanding of the many facets of urban ministry, invest in a one-year subscription to *Urban Mission*, published by Westminster Theological Seminary in Philadelphia. For $10 you will be informed and challenged by articles like "Urban Poor-ology: A Theology of Ministry to the World's Urban Poor," "The Rise of Spiritism in North America," and "Personal Evangelism in the Inner City."

3. *Listen*. Raymond Bakke, a Baptist pastor with extensive experience in inner-city Chicago, delivered two eye-opening messages at a church growth symposium hosted by Concordia Seminary, St. Louis. For $3 each you can hear "Challenges of Urbanization to Mission Thinking and Strategy" and "Strategies and Models for Urban Evangelism." These messages are great!

4. *Look*. Obtain a listing of the films and videos available from Lutheran World Relief. Choose two or three and share them with your church or with a group of friends. The films will be more worthwhile than most of those available at the local video store.

5. *Converse*. While informally chatting with members of your church, mention the ethnic peoples that are found in your community. Listen for what attitudes are expressed regarding these groups. Determine to what degree parishioners are open to befriending and ministering to them.

6. *Pray*. Keep an antenna up for people in your community who belong

to other ethnic groups or religions. As you become aware of them, add them to your prayer list. If your community is purely monocultural, then pray for God to bring someone whose presence will add variety.

Chapter 6
The Cultural Mosaic

The Last Eighteen Inches

The preceding chapter encouraged North American Christians to participate in the challenge of God's worldwide mission, especially where there are outreach possibilities near enough for them to participate personally. We hope many people will respond to this proposal with enthusiasm. However, even for those who are eager for such cross-cultural involvement, nagging fears may arise, the fear of all that is strange and foreign, the fear of culture shock.

To enjoy watching a missionary's slides is one thing; to actually dwell in the alien surroundings where he lives is another. To sightsee in a foreign land is one thing; to become a permanent resident there is another. To dream about witnessing to your Hindu or Hispanic neighbors is one thing; to really share Christ with them in an effective and understandable manner is another.

While cross-cultural activities have a built-in exotic appeal, at the same time they cause us a degree of discomfort, depending on the strangeness of the new environment and culture in which we find ourselves. Veteran missionary David Hesselgrave describes the difficulty:

> Before missionaries go to a foreign country the first time, they tend to think primarily of the great distance they must travel to get to their field of labor. . . . But once they arrive on the field, they begin to realize that in this modern age it is nothing to travel great distances. The great problem to be faced is the last eighteen inches! What a shock! (Hesselgrave 1978, 69).

Rookie missionary Richard Stokes describes the shock of the last eighteen inches upon his arrival in Togo, West Africa:

> I thought that I had stepped onto the set of the old Humphrey Bogart movie, *Casablanca*. . . .
> It seemed as if everything and everyone was in motion—couples out for an evening stroll, young people walking back and forth under street lamps reading their lessons for school. In the darkness, radios mixed the music of West Africa with the odors of kerosene lamps and meat cooking over open fires. . . .
> At six the next morning we drove through the same streets, now crowded with honking cars, bikes and motorbikes, taxis and buses bulging with people—people walking in every direction, with loads on their heads and laughter in their lavish greetings.

We stopped at a narrow, unpaved side street. Chickens scratched in the dirt while goats ambled along the quiet street just a few yards from the busy thoroughfare. The man seated behind the picnic-style table greeted us with a smile and outstretched arms, inviting all 10 of us to be seated around him. . . .

Breakfast was cooked over an open charcoal fire. Bowls, plates and spoons were dipped in a bucket of water and set before us. . . . Seeing my family seated there, against that background, I must confess, I was overcome with doubt and began to wonder, "What have I done?" (Stokes 1987, 3).

What do we mean by the last eighteen inches? At that distance we realize that people are culturally different from us. We can no longer deceive ourselves that they are really just like us, except that they wear different clothes. No, people really are different, because cultures are unique. The last eighteen inches are the hardest. This is as true for professional missionaries as it is for Christians at home who wish to share Christ across a cultural barrier. The missionary in Germany, befriending and witnessing to Turkish factory workers, must learn to deal with the last eighteen inches. The layperson in Toronto or Tulsa who wishes to befriend and share Christ with Muslim neighbors must learn to deal with the last eighteen inches.

The problem of culture is one of the reasons that Stephen Neill writes: "Christian missionary work is the most difficult thing in the world. It is surprising that it should ever have been attempted" (Neill 1970, 24). Recognizing this fact, many Christians hesitate from associating with people from another ethnic background.

There is no denying that cross-cultural outreach is difficult and taxing. But the joy of seeing people come to know Christ is unparalleled. In this chapter we shall candidly discuss some of the difficulties and obstacles in communicating Christ cross-culturally. We shall also underscore and affirm the corresponding joy that results from confronting and overcoming the difficulties.

Language

The Need to Learn the Language of Others

The most obvious cultural difference is language. If you get to those last eighteen inches and cannot communicate verbally, how helpless you feel grunting and gesturing to get your point across! The frustration is multiplied when the message you wish to convey is the saving Word of God. Missionary Ron Astalos described his feelings after his first night in a Japanese household:

We passed the time by looking at the souvenirs and other odds and ends which we had brought with us on the plane. Also with us were three children, friends of the family. One of them picked up my picture of Christ and in Japanese said, "Who is this?" I understood that much Japanese, but my Japanese is so limited that all I could say was "It is Jesus Christ." What a

91

tremendous opportunity to tell the plan of salvation to these children who did not even recognize a picture of Christ let alone know of the eternal life which He offers them. Yet I had to sit there on the floor virtually speechless because of the language barrier (Astalos 1962, 1–2).

The same hurdle often exists in North America. Unfortunately, many Christians decline to make the sacrifice of learning another language. Walter DeMoss, veteran missionary in West Africa, laments this reluctance:

> More than ever people in the U.S. have an opportunity to meet people from Hispanic, Oriental, and other cultures, but few people really dig into the situation and try to relate to these people in a culturally meaningful way. I used to correspond with a young pastor who had received a call to a small Texas town where I guess a large percentage of the people spoke only Spanish or just a bit of English. I challenged him. Why don't you learn Spanish and really do a job? No way! He soon took a call to a bigger and better place where people spoke English. I can't imagine the apostle Paul letting a little thing like language get in his way. The Lord gave us the intelligence to leap over the language barrier, but we are afraid to try. Paul says in Romans 10 that people can't believe unless they have heard the word, and they can't hear if no one speaks it to them, and, I would add, they will never be spoken to if we do not jump the language barrier and speak the precious gospel to them in a language they can understand.

DeMoss's words may strike North Americans as incredibly optimistic. "A little thing like language," he says, when experience tells us it is an insurmountable obstacle. Many of us know language only "as a high-school subject like trigonometry, invented apparently just to harass people" (Stafford 1984, 80). Some of us gave up after Spanish I or II. Others battled on to French III or German IV, but to no avail. We conjugated verbs, declined nouns, and memorized vocabulary, and in the end, we could only carry on a stumbling conversation in that foreign tongue. Meanwhile, over half of the world's population speaks more than one language. It is little wonder that the rest of the world jokes about U.S. citizens:

> A person who speaks three languages is trilingual.
> A person who speaks two languages is bilingual. And what do you call someone who speaks only one language?
> An American.

In light of our failure to learn other lingoes, we try to think up ways to avoid this challenge. One way is to blame God. The argument goes like this: The story of the Tower of Babel (Gen. 11:1–9) demonstrates that diversity of language is all God's doing. He placed that curse on mankind so that we would each remain isolated on our own linguistic islands. So who am I to spoil God's plans by learning one of those barbaric tongues?

Those who harbor such thoughts base their argument on the assumption that the Tower of Babel is the sole cause of language diversity. This is not so. Even if the Tower of Babel episode had not occurred, there would still be many, many languages in this world, for the simple reason that languages are constantly changing. If two groups of people who speak the same tongue are isolated from each other for generations, they will eventually speak two different languages. So let us not blame God for all the multiplicity of languages. Yes, He got the process rolling by confusing the builders of Babel, but it would have happened eventually anyhow. Furthermore, we know that God wants His people to bridge the linguistic gap. Otherwise, the Holy Spirit would not have bothered to give the apostles the gift of speaking in other languages on the day of Pentecost.

Another way we try to avoid the discomfort of language study is to assume that everyone else should learn English. I recall a conversation with a solid churchgoer who was discussing the work being done by a missionary friend in Africa.

"Chuck and Lucy have had to go through such pains to learn that strange language," he said. "Wouldn't it have been easier for the people in that tribe to have learned English?"

"Well, let's think about that," I responded cautiously. "How many people are in their tribe?"

"About 200,000."

"Which do you think would be easier, to teach only two people a new language or to teach 200,000 folks a new language?"

"Oh, I see what you mean. It would take almost forever for Chuck and Lucy to teach English to such a multitude. If they tried, they would become English teachers instead of gospel preachers."

Martin Luther recognized the urgency for us to take the step of learning languages when he declared:

> I do not at all agree with those who cling to one language and despise all others. I would rather train such youth and folk who could also be of service to Christ in foreign lands and be able to converse with the natives there (Leupold 1965, 63).

Keys to Learning a Language

Thus, the burden of learning languages rests on the Christian who desires to share his faith cross-culturally. How can we hope to succeed when so many of us have a history of language frustration? Perhaps in your school days you failed to learn to speak another language. So did I. I faked my way through both French and German with paltry conversational ability to show for my efforts. Maybe you have concluded that you do not have "that special gift" for languages. I suspected I did not have it either. Perhaps you have concluded that for you language is an insurmountable barrier. I know the feeling.

But I have a surprise for you. Most people have more aptitude for learning a language than they imagine. The barrier is not insurmountable. David wrote, "With my God I can scale a wall" (Ps. 18:29). Trusting in the Lord to guide you and using proper techniques, you *can* become fluent. Now that I am bilingual, I know this to be true. Let me share with you some of the key

93

factors which have helped me and many others "scale the wall."

The first factor is motivation. Where there is a will, there is a way. Where there is no will, there is no way to learn another tongue. Few high school and college students are highly motivated to master a language. It is just another obligation to be endured before they can don their cap and gown. Perhaps they begin their studies with enthusiasm, but enthusiasm is not enough; it is only an emotion that comes and goes. Motivation is of another breed. "Motivation is a determination which results in a *decision of the will*— 'I *will* learn.' The 'I will' is far more important in language learning than the I.Q." (Brewster and Brewster 1976, 2).

Therefore, do not judge your present ability to learn a language on past experiences when you may have lacked motivation. If you determine to learn Spanish or Vietnamese in order to meet people on their own turf and to speak Christ's love to them, what higher motive is there than that? With this noble purpose, the Holy Spirit will empower you to climb over the wall.

A second factor is environment. I did not master a language until I lived among people who spoke it. This is the great shortcoming of our formal language education: we usually have no one with whom to "*parlez-vous.*" You see, the key to language is not grammar and textbooks. The key is the people that speak the language. If your goal is merely to learn a language, you might fail; but if your purpose is to establish friendships with people, you will succeed in learning their language. So find people with whom to speak. Perhaps you can establish a relationship with someone else, in which you teach them English and they teach you Italian or Cambodian or Hindi. To guide you in your environmental language learning, obtain a copy of the book *Language Acquisition Made Practical* by Tom and Elizabeth Brewster. You will find this to be a practical, comprehensive, and humorous guide to help learn any language by befriending people and taking an interest in their culture.

A third factor that contributes to language learning is the willingness to swallow all your pride and actually speak the language, no matter how many mistakes you make. You already did it once, when you learned your native tongue. Babbling incessantly, you practiced the sounds without embarrassment, because you were only a toddler. After age 12, language learning becomes much harder, because teenagers are ruled by intense peer pressure that dictates, "At all costs, don't put your foot in your mouth! Don't make a fool of yourself in front of everyone!"

Adults who are studying a language are often dominated by similar self-consciousness. To learn a language you have to murder it—over and over again. It was the only way when you were a toddler; it is the only way at any age. "You do not learn a language once, but a hundred times. The first ninety-nine times you learn a word you forget it. . . . [Y]our mind moves so slowly you can hear it rusting" (Stafford 1984, 88). Nevertheless, there are fringe benefits to all the agony involved. You will learn humility as never before and develop a great sense of humor. Consider, for example, the following stories told by Todd Roeske who served as a Lutheran Youth Volunteer missionary in Taiwan:

> There is nothing that I can think of which is quite as humbling as learning a new language. Less than a year ago, I sat in classes which discussed (in English) the theories of 20th century political thought and the history of theology. Now I struggle to tell a store clerk that I want to buy a pen that doesn't make splotches. (How do you say "splotches" in Chinese, anyway?)
>
> I finally felt like I was beginning to make progress in Chinese. I had a couple of conversations in which I actually understood what the subject was, and I had discovered that I could read over 75 of those random scribbles which Chinese people call characters. "This Chinese stuff isn't so hard after all," I proudly thought as I boarded the elevator. Then I noticed a little six-year-old girl standing next to me. She was holding her school book—it was exactly the book which I am studying. So much for pride.
>
> As all good Chinese students do, I happily greet passersby with a friendly "Ni hau" (How are you?) and "Dzau" (Good morning) on my way to class. It is quite typical for a Chinese person to excitedly chatter a stream of unintelligible syllables back at me in reply. I respond in the best way I know how: My face contorts in puzzlement and I grunt, "Huh?" The Chinese person will then respond in a much slower version of his previous chatter. After several repetitions and various gestures I realize that he has said, "Your Chinese is really very good." "Oh, thank you," I mutter, as we both go on our ways feeling quite embarrassed.

Language: The Key to the Heart

Yes, humility and a sense of humor are certainly fringe benefits, but the greatest benefit is knowing another person's heart language. Heart language is one's mother tongue. It plumbs the depths of people's emotions and touches their heartstrings. Lutherans of northern European heritage are familiar with heart language. How we once clung to the speech of the homeland!

In his yarns about Lake Wobegon, humorist Garrison Keillor often expresses the feelings of Norwegian immigrants who learned English in middle age and could never be quite so intelligent or romantic or brave in that borrowed language (Keillor 1985, 79).

Missionary Phil Sipes in Ghana, West Africa, attests to the compelling nature of heart language in regard to religion:

> We began using the Bimoba New Testament translation in our Bible classes and sermon classes. Before, those who did not speak or read English did not come to our classes because they could not fully take part in the Bible studies since we only had English Bibles. Or when they did come, they would look bored. . . . But now, they could read the Bible in their own language and add comments and take part in the discussion. Their eyes were full of curiosity and joy, seeing God's word in a language that they could read and understand (Sipes 1988, 2).

The concept of heart language reveals why Christians endure the rigors and humiliation of learning another language. Every soul needs to be opened to the saving power of the Gospel, and "language is the key to the souls of men" (Vicedom 1961, 13). Once a heart is opened, all the trial and heartache is diminished, just as a woman forgets her travail when her newborn child is placed in her arms.

One person who eventually experienced such joy was Ron Astalos, who was quoted earlier regarding his first frustrating night in Japan. However, during missionary Astalos' 14 years in the Land of the Rising Sun, he saw the blessed results of "scaling the wall" of language as he was used by God to lead many individuals to Christ. Rejoice with him as he relates the following intriguing story:

> In the summer of 1962 we had just received our call to Japan and immediately began sorting through all our belongings. . . . We left behind everything we could. I felt a little guilty leaving my trumpet in the pile destined for Japan, but I couldn't bring myself to leave it behind. Now I see what the Lord had in mind when He led me to bring it along. . . .
>
> . . . [J]ust this week I received a letter from Miss Ikue Ozaki. She wanted to share with us the good news that she was baptized on Christmas Eve [1967]. Let me tell you what my trumpet had to do with her baptism.
>
> When we arrived in Tokyo in 1962, like all new missionaries, I spent my first two years in full time Japanese language study. During this time I wanted a chance to make more Japanese acquaintances and also to put my language to use. So I looked around for an amateur orchestra in which I could play my trumpet. . . . In one orchestra, the trumpet player next to me was a young man called Ozaki-san, an excellent trumpet player. I only attended a few rehearsals and then for some reason I changed orchestras. At that time I wrote you asking you to pray that the Lord might use even this experience in His own time and way.
>
> At the end of my two years of language study I won the Fifth Annual International Japanese Language Speech Contest. As a result I appeared on several TV programs. Immediately after the program the Ozaki family called us to say they saw me on TV. I had just begun my work at Azabu Seisen Lutheran Church in Tokyo so I invited them to church and to my English class.
>
> Miss Ozaki, a high school student, did come to my English class, but not to church. We had chorus practice after the English class so she joined the chorus. . . .Ozaki-san loved to sing so much that she decided to join the chorus of our largest congregation in Tokyo. But she had never shown any interest in attending church or Bible study. I wondered what would become of her.
>
> Now suddenly to hear that she is baptized is thrilling news! The Lord did have a plan in leading me to take my trumpet to Japan. He did use my orchestra experience, my TV appearance, my English class and the chorus to bring this precious soul into His kingdom (Astalos 1968, 1–2).

In a world with 5,455 languages (Johnstone, 1986, 32), we cannot keep making excuses for our monolingual myopia. Thank God, we do not have to learn all 5,455! Learning only one would be sufficient to bridge the gap to a different ethnic group. If the Holy Spirit compels you to tackle a language, be assured that you can do it. You just need the right ingredients: (1) the right motivation, to share Christ; (2) the proper environment, people with whom to converse in your new language; and (3) a healthy dose of Spirit-inspired humility to help you overcome your self-consciousness. With these factors in your favor, you will find David's boast to be true: "With my God I can scale a wall" (Ps. 18:29).

The Cultural Mosaic

How marvelous it is to reach the point at which you can carry on lengthy conversations in a new language without getting a headache! Then, just when you imagine that you almost understand your new culture, something strange happens. You begin to notice a thousand little things that you do not comprehend at all, and it dawns on you that there is more to culture than language.

This realization is something like putting together a thousand-piece jigsaw puzzle. You dig and delve through the cardboard flotsam prospecting for the four corner pieces and all the other outer pieces with one flat side. Then you mix and match them, twist and turn them, until you have the outer frame of the puzzle in place. "Good job!" you congratulate yourself, but then you remember that a mountain of over 900 pieces, the most challenging part of the puzzle, still remains.

Learning a culture is similar. Grasping the language is like constructing the frame of the jigsaw puzzle. It is a significant accomplishment, but it is not the whole job. This does not mean that language study is a waste of time. Without the language—and the friendships you establish as you learn it—you will not be able to piece together the rest of the puzzle.

Now let us alter and improve the metaphor. From our perspective another culture is like a puzzle, because it confuses us. To the people of that culture, however, it makes perfect sense. They see their culture, not as a puzzle, but as a mosaic of interrelated customs, objects, ideas, and values. The more we study a second culture, the more it changes from being a puzzle to a mosaic with intricate design. Although, as outsiders, we may never fully understand the mosaic of another culture, still, as we make the effort to understand and accept the culture, we will be better equipped to share the Word of our Savior within that culture.

Just as there are different colors in a mosaic, so there are different features in a culture. Here are some of them:
1. Objects and materials—what is used and collected
2. Cognitive processes—ways of thinking, forms of logic
3. Linguistic forms—ways of expressing ideas
4. Art and media—ways of channeling a message
5. Behavioral patterns—ways of acting
6. Social structures—ways of interacting
7. Decision methods—ways of making choices and changes
8. Values—what is good or bad

9. Beliefs—what is true or false
10. World view—ways of perceiving reality
(Hesselgrave 1978, 120 and Bunkowske 1988a, 8)

This list reveals that there is a great deal to keep in mind when we are relating to people of other ethnic groups. Let us consider some typical examples of the variety to be found in the cultural mosaic.

Linguistic forms include more than verbal communication. Body language is equally important. The French gesture in French. The Quechua Indians of the Andes Mountains gesture in Quechua. "To be bilingual means to know two languages of gestures as well as two languages of words" (Hesselgrave, 1978, 296). How can you learn body language? Keep your eyes open and do not hesitate to ask people to explain their gestures. Then try using these motions yourself (if they are not obscene). Just like speaking a language, the movements will feel uncomfortable at first, but after a while they will be second nature.

Behavioral patterns also require much attention, as British missionary Michael Goldsmith illustrates:

> It was a beautiful moonlit tropical evening, and we were holding an open-air service for Malay people. This was a regular weekly event and the local people were getting to know us. I was thrilled to have an opportunity to use my few sentences of Malay. . . . Wherever the opportunity occurred, I handed out tracts. Being used to dealing cards with my left hand, I did the same with these leaflets, and was blissfully unaware of the local culture which considered the public use of the left hand to be offensive. A middle-aged man took a tract, but his scowl showed his displeasure; I thought he must be a strong Muslim and therefore unhappy with this Christian witness.
>
> During the following week I read in a book that Malays do not use their left hand publicly, and therefore I began to use only my right hand at the next open-air service. The same Malay man approached me. "I am glad to see that you have learnt some manners at last," he announced haughtily and stalked off into the night. I knew then that all those previous weeks I had been saying through my actions that the gospel of Christ is offensive. Through cultural failure I was making Christ more of a mystery than was really necessary (Goldsmith 1976, 126).

Tales such as these may cause us to freeze for fear of making a mistake. The main thing is to keep learning and be willing to alter your behavior to the local customs. Once Michael Goldsmith discovered what was expected, he made the necessary adjustments. "When in Rome. . . ."

Another cultural difference which causes great havoc is the attitude toward time. Very few non-Western cultures have as sensitive a sense of time as we do. "In most countries people consider us . . . handcuffed by our wristwatch to a relentless time schedule" (George Patterson 1977, 113). No wonder, then, that non-Western tardiness frustrates us. One spring, missionary to Venezuela Mike Brockman was upset because his confirmation students kept showing up later and later for their lessons. He chided them every week to gather at 6 p.m., but to no avail. Finally, it dawned on him that they always arrived an hour before sundown. According to his digital wristwatch they were late; according to their clock, the sun, they were very punctual. With that realization Mike adjusted to their schedule.

The most amazing features of the cultural mosaic are worldviews or ways that we perceive the world around us. A worldview is the pair of tinted glasses through which one mentally looks at the universe. In order to relate to people of another culture, we need to understand their worldview. In a sense, we need to remove our tinted glasses and put on theirs, so that we can perceive things as they do.

The importance of worldview cannot be overestimated. For example, knowing that the Japanese are a highly technological people, we may mistakenly assume that their worldview leaves little room for superstitious beliefs. Wisconsin Synod missionary Glen Hieb provides ample evidence to the contrary:

> In Japan the majority of the people do not put their trust in the risen Lord. Most of the people live a very superstitious life. Millions of Japanese put their faith in a lunar system borrowed long ago from China. This system has a six day cycle of lucky days, unlucky days and so-so days. Good fortune may come in the morning, only to disappear in the afternoon. Get sick on an unpropitious day, and the illness is certain to linger. Pick a wrong day for a funeral, and another burial will soon follow. . . .
>
> When Japanese build houses, they see to it that no gate, door, or window faces the NE because demons come from that direction. In naming their children, parents count the brush strokes required to write the characters, making sure they do not add up to unlucky numbers. . . .
>
> No sensible politician starts a campaign without first painting in the left eye of a dauruma, a stubby red doll symbolizing good luck. After victory, the right eye is filled in too.
>
> Half of all Japanese believe they are afflicted with unlucky years. For the men the unlucky years are their 25th and 42nd. The women consider their 19th and 33rd years to be most unlucky (*Winning Souls* 1987, 18-19).

The lenses of the Japanese worldview have a different tint from ours. When we understand how they (or any other group) look at the world, we will be able to communicate Biblical truth to them in a more effective manner.

We have looked at only a few examples of cultural variety. If culture is a mosaic, how do we learn to understand and appreciate it? To a degree we can learn through reading. A subscription to *National Geographic* will be a good investment, and geography books from the library can inform us, but the best way to learn is through meeting and relating to people of another culture. That will take some effort, especially for those who are used to seeking refuge in the confines of the familiar.

As you venture out into relationships with people from other cultures, expect to wrestle with anger and depression. Veteran missionary to Venezuela Douglas Johnstone, explains why:

> The biggest problem you will have in dealing with people of another

culture is anger. You will become exasperated that people do not do things the way you expect, according to your preconceived, culturally determined ways of thinking. This anger often leads to depression, because as a Christian you know that your rage is inconsistent with your desire to share Christ with these people. In order to overcome anger and depression, you need to fall in love with the people. This is not a blind, romantic love that ignores problems and weaknesses, but the love of a mature courtship leading to eventual marriage, a love that learns to understand and to work through problem areas together.

Yes, the difficulties of relating cross-culturally are very real, but the benefits are just as real. To see the beauty of the cultural mosaic, throw yourself into relationships with ethnic peoples, into their world. When you do so, you will find a special joy awaiting you. Becky Hsiao (Gimbel) expressed that joy poetically in an address given at the consecration service of 12 Volunteer Youth Ministers headed for Japan and Taiwan to teach English and to witness:

WELCOME

We welcome you to Taiwan, to Japan.
We welcome all of you—not all in terms of numbers, but *all* in terms
of all of each of you.
We welcome your whole person.

We welcome your eyes . . .
to see the hunger for love,
to see the yearning for fulfillment,
to see the love between brothers and sisters of different races,
to see the "new creation in Christ" emerge after a friend's
Baptism,
"to see the hope to which He has called you, the riches of His
inheritance and His great power" (Eph. 1:18–19).

We welcome your ears . . .
to hear the strange words of another language that slowly take on
meaning,
to hear the questions of students who are asking you about your
faith,
to hear the words of love and forgiveness that go with you across
the world,
"to hear the voice of the Shepherd and follow Him"
(John 10:3–4).

We welcome your mouth . . .
to open up and eat those new and "interesting" foods,
to open up and smile encouragement to your English students,
to open up and share the "hope that is within you" (1 Peter 3:15).
to open up and eat the Body and Blood of our Savior.

We welcome your hands . . .
> to reach out and grasp the chopsticks for your meals,
> to reach out and lift up the discouraged student,
> to reach out and write letters to prayer partners,
> to reach out and wrap hands of love around lonely people,
> to reach out and touch in the name of Jesus.

We welcome your feet . . .
> to walk in markets and shops with the Japanese and Chinese,
> to walk to the church leading a friend,
> to walk the road of loneliness and questioning to find Jesus beside you,
> "to walk in the light as He is in the light and in fellowship with one another" (1 John 1:7).

We welcome . . .
> You whom God created and knit together in your mother's womb,
> You whom God called to be His sons and daughters through Baptism,
> You whom He called to offer your bodies as living sacrifices.

We welcome you . . . ALL OF YOU!

Communicating Christ Cross-culturally

The greatest challenge in cross-cultural work is to convey the Gospel of Jesus Christ so that it will be understood clearly by the hearers. This is no easy task because of syncretism (the tendency of listeners to bend a new teaching in order to make it fit in with their present beliefs). Even New Testament missionaries had this problem:

> In Lystra there sat a man crippled in his feet, who was lame from birth and had never walked. He listened to Paul as he was speaking. Paul looked directly at him, saw that he had faith to be healed and called out, "Stand up on your feet!" At that, the man jumped up and began to walk.
> When the crowd saw what Paul had done, they shouted in the Lycaonian language, "The gods have come down to us in human form!" Barnabas they called Zeus, and Paul they called Hermes because he was the chief speaker. The priest of Zeus, whose temple was just outside the city, brought bulls and wreaths to the city gates because he and the crowd wanted to offer sacrifices to them.
> But when the apostles Barnabas and Paul heard of this, they tore their clothes and rushed out into the crowd, shouting: "Men, why are you doing this? We too are only men, human like you. We are bringing you good news, telling you to turn from these worthless things to the living God, who made heaven and earth and sea and everything in them" (Acts 14:8–15).

Ever since the days of Paul and Barnabas, Christians who wish to communicate Christ cross-culturally have been met with misunderstandings. For example, missionaries to India have been held in low esteem by high-caste Hindus, who consider the missionaries to be outcastes. The bigotry of the caste system is even directed at Christ Himself. High-caste Hindus take offense at the fact that Jesus was a carpenter and many of His disciples were fishermen—both groups being inferior castes in the Hindu system (Kane 1986, 120).

Similar cross-cultural confusion arises regarding the essential Christian concept of salvation by grace, not by works. Dr. Thomas Hale, medical missionary to Nepal, speaks of the mindset of the Hindus he serves:

> Most of our patients have no sense of gratitude for our services; instead, they expect that *we* be grateful to them for providing us with an opportunity to gain merit for ourselves. This is why "thank you" is so rarely heard in Nepal; in fact, the Nepali language has no word for it (Hale, 1986, 75).

Muslims are just as confused on this issue. "Some who work among Muslims have tried to show the love of Christ by caring for sick people, helping the women, repairing motorbikes for the men—utterly giving of themselves—only to hear, 'Oh, he was just trying to gain favor with his God' " (Shelley 1977, 108).

What a conundrum! Christ commanded us to love, but, in the above cases, when love is expressed, people assume that salvation is by works. Surely, "the god of this age [Satan] has blinded the minds of unbelievers, so that they cannot see the light of the gospel of the glory of Christ, who is the image of God" (2 Cor. 4:4). Those who have wrestled with such frustrations can identify with missionary to the Philippines Rosemary Althoff, who confessed, "We felt like we were scattering seeds in an unknown field in the dark, and it was difficult to know what would grow or where."

Yet even with so many strikes against us, there is evidence that it is possible to communicate the Gospel across cultural barriers. The first reason for hope is that the Holy Spirit has already successfully communicated Christ to thousands of people groups. Christianity did not start here in North America. God caused it to arise in the ancient Middle East among people very different from you. Even though you know precious little about that land and culture, the Holy Spirit was able to communicate the good news to you. What a miracle! It is a miracle which the Holy Spirit has worked in culture after culture, so that today the worship of the Triune God is the most universal of all the religions on this planet. A missionary in Africa expresses this fact well:

> I am the son of Abraham. Yet how different in physical terms we are! His appearance, culture, customs, and manner of worship were undoubtedly quite different from mine. Yet, I am his descendant, a fellow heir. And so is anyone else who believes the gospel, no matter how weird he or she may seem to me, no matter how different. We are all brothers and sisters with one Lord.

This fact is true of all believers, whether they are from North America, Peru, South Africa, or Vietnam. "Those who believe are children of Abraham" (Gal. 3:7), because the Holy Spirit has bridged the cultural gap to reach them with the message of Christ's salvation.

The second reason for hope is that culture, when viewed properly, is not a barrier but a bridge for communicating the Gospel. Every cultural mosaic contains some parts which can be used for conveying Christian truth. For example, in 1867, Norwegian missionary Lars Skrefsrud discovered that the Santal tribe (located in present-day Bangladesh) believed in an all-powerful creator whom they called *Thakur Jiu,* "genuine god." According to their tradition, the tribe had experienced much misery ever since they had turned away from this god to lesser gods. Skrefsrud used this name, Thakur Jiu, for God the Father who was calling the Santals to return to Him through the reconciliation of Jesus Christ. Thousands were converted (Strom 1987, 255).

We need to keep our eyes open to similar parallels between the Bible and a given culture. Such parallels serve as audio-visual aids by which God's eternal truths can be communicated to different peoples. The audio-visual aids can be as significant as the word for god, in the case above, or as commonplace and seemingly inconsequential as a bag. The Kisi people of Liberia have a proverb: "An empty bag cannot stand." An empty person cannot stand either, at least not for very long. Therefore, the Kisi Christians say that Christmas means "filling your bag," because Christ has filled them with His many blessings (Roegner 1986, 3).

The net bag is a common means of carrying heavy loads in Papua New Guinea. The bag rests on the bearer's back, while a strap fits over the forehead to assist in supporting the heavy load. Seeing people (mostly women) carry heavy loads in this manner, artist-missionary Sylvia Zabransky Hemmann had an idea. She sketched a net bag hanging from a cross, thus symbolizing that Papuans can bring all their troubles, problems, and cares to Jesus, who bore their sins on the cross. Sylvia's design has become a common symbol in the Gutnius Lutheran Church.

Another example of culturally adapted imagery is the logo of *Arrow,* the Montana Indian Ministry newsletter. The logo combines (1) the crossed arrows representing peace, (2) the butterfly symbolizing eternal life, and (3) the cross of the Lord Jesus. This combination of Indian and Christian symbols conveys Biblical truths in terms which American Indians can understand.

In Japan the tying of a sash can be a means of proclaiming the Christian faith:

> "Oh, *Sensei!* (teacher) what kind of *obi* (sash) shall I tie for my baptism? Should I tie in the manner of a funeral for the death of my former sinful self? Or for a marriage as I join myself to Christ? Or for the joyous occasion of a birth, even though I am old, as I am reborn in Christ through the water of baptism?" Dear Mrs. Hashizumi, 63-year-old grandmother, was asking these questions shortly before her baptism on Pentecost. Did she ask them in the privacy of the missionary's study, or in the seclusion of the church building? No, she was talking to her companion, a Sunday school teacher,

as they were traveling together in a bus on their way into the heart of the city. And all the passengers on the bus heard her witness. Some laughed, of course, but others were quick to hear and slow to laugh (Dorn 1962, 28-29).

One of the most powerful aspects of a culture is its music. In fact, the influence of music is so strong that often missionaries assume that their style of music is the only proper one to use for Christian worship. But did God really intend for believers from six continents all to be singing translations of Western hymns? If God had intended all the world to use only one style of music, He would have seen to it that the music of the Jewish psalms would have been preserved along with the words. It is certainly appropriate for us to share some of the outstanding hymns of our culture with other peoples, but they should be allowed to compose their own so that the musical arts may blossom with Christian themes. Eugene Bunkowske commented regarding the development of Christian music among the Yala people of Nigeria, West Africa:

> Almost immediately from the beginning Ferdinand took selected Scripture portions and put them to Yala music. Soon the children were singing that music in the playgrounds in the evening. Soon it moved out from Okpoma to other towns. From town to town as the Word of the Lord grew.
>
> I knew very little about musicology. I was a bit worried when the people began to sing these songs all over Yala and so I said to Ferdinand one day, "How do you choose the music for these hymns?" By that time I understood the language well enough to know that there were songs about head-hunting and all kinds of songs, both bad and good. So I asked Ferdinand, "How do you choose the tunes?" Ferdinand said to me, "Well, there are some tunes that I do not use. When you hear that tune, then there are certain thoughts and ideas that are automatically connected with that musical tune. If those thoughts are non-Scriptural or against the Word of God, I do not use that music. If the thought-connotation in the music is positive or neutral, I use that tune."
>
> And there it was. The Word of God moved out through music. In every culture that I know, music is a powerful message-projector. If the proper indigenous music is chosen, the capacity for the message to move out is much enhanced. If non-indigenous music is chosen, the natural movement of the Gospel is often repressed (Bunkowske 1988b, 78-79).

The Scriptures often sound the refrain "Sing to the Lord a new song" (Ps. 149:1). This will surely occur as Christian composers arise in new cultures that have not known the glories of our God. We Western Christians like to dream about being in heaven singing new songs from the pen of Johann Sebastian Bach and other sainted musicians with whom we will share eternity. I expect that will indeed occur, but we may also join in praising the Most High in songs written by believing composers from every tribe, tongue, people, and nation.

Cultural adaptation is also essential in the use of mass media. Too many media ministries are simply a rehashing of the communication forms common in North America without thoughtful adaptation to the local culture. The "Lutheran Hour" of the Lutheran Church-Missouri Synod has been praised for its cultural sensitivity: "As a result of careful study and implementation the format has been changed in the case of many cultures from the sermonic one so familiar to North American listeners to drama, documentary, story-telling, and music with commentary formats" (Hesselgrave 1978, 403).

The point of all these examples is that sensitivity to culture will help Christians overcome the barriers and discover the bridges to people. Sensitivity entails much study and observation. Missionaries have not always been so sensitive. Sometimes they have actively attacked the native culture, mistakenly assuming that there was nothing good or useful to be found among unbelievers. In these cases, the missionaries were like housing developers who assume that, before they can build, all the trees on a piece of land must be bulldozed. Today's cross-cultural witnesses are learning that their purpose is to preserve as much of the recipients' culture as possible. They work like a building contractor with an aesthetic sense and an environmental conscience, sparing as many trees as possible to grace the landscape.

Sometimes the key factor is to discover what the cultural barrier is and then remove it. A case in point is the work of Tribal Missions, a mission society formed by Indian Christians. The first people they sought to reach were the Cholanaikkans, a naked, fair-skinned tribe that lived nearby in the Indian state of Kerala. The Cholanaikkans were very primitive; they did not bathe, groom their hair and teeth, nor cook. After several attempts to locate the tribe in the wooded hills they were known to inhabit, the Indian missionaries finally made contact. However, the Cholanaikkans fled from them in fear, hiding in their caves and refusing all attempts to coax them out.

After much discussion the missionaries conjectured that their clothes might be a barrier to the naked Cholanaikkans. So they decided to experiment. Removing all but the clothing around their waists, they approached the primitive tribesmen once again. Amazingly, it worked, for some of the braver men began to communicate with them. In time, the missionaries won their confidence and shared God's Word with them. Within three years over half the Cholanaikkans came to confess Jesus Christ as Lord and were baptized (Wagner 1983, 118–19).

These wise Indian missionaries used the "save the trees" strategy. Looking for a bridge to the Cholanaikkans, they surmised that they would not begin to bear fruit among this tribe until they stripped down to their "Fruit of the Looms." This is the kind of adaptability to which first-century missionary Paul referred when he wrote, "I have become all things to all men so that by all possible means I might save some. I do all this for the sake of the gospel, that I may share in its blessings" (1 Cor. 9:22–23).

The Bible Viewed through Other Cultures

A marvelous benefit of involvement in God's mission is a fuller understanding of the Christian faith. There are many Biblical themes that we Westerners tend to overlook, but through contact with another culture these themes appear in all their power and beauty. Missionary Roger Buck explains how living in Togo, West Africa, has helped him fathom the significance of the story of the Samaritan woman at the well:

> Women in Togo continually find themselves at the water hole searching for that precious commodity, whereas in our culture one hardly even realizes its importance. Jesus offers her the greatest gift in the world, living water, that is, eternal life. To never have to walk many miles, or to not wait for a dry hole to fill up with a little water is significant for the women here in Togo. The picture of having all we need to live eternally is vividly portrayed.

Dr. Eugene Bunkowske, professor of missions at Concordia Theological Seminary in Fort Wayne, Indiana, served among the Yala people of southeastern Nigeria. When Bunkowske had learned the Yala language and was about to begin translating the Bible, he asked his national assistant, "Ferdinand, this translation project will take many years. If we had time to translate only one book of the Word of God, which book would you propose?"

Think about that. It is an intriguing question. Which book would be the most useful to the Yala people? Bunkowske expected an answer such as Romans, or one of the gospels, because in North America we tend to introduce unbelievers to those books first. But without hesitation Ferdinand declared, "The book of Jonah!"

"Jonah?" Bunkowske responded in surprise. "Why?"

"There are several reasons. First of all, when Jonah ran away God followed him out to sea and brought him back. That shows that God's power is not limited to just one geographic area. The Yala need to know that God is the only divine ruler in all the earth."

"After the Gentile sailors tossed Jonah into the sea, they worshipped Jehovah. This shows that everyone can worship Him, even the Yala. Then God finally succeeded in getting Jonah to warn the Ninevites. God's concern for that group of people reveals that He loves all peoples and is deeply concerned about them. He sends missionaries like Jonah to teach them the truth."

"Just as I and others have come to the Yala," Bunkowske interjected.

"Exactly! My last reason for choosing Jonah is that God forgave the Ninevites when they repented. That will show the Yala that He is ready and willing to forgive all who turn from their evil ways."

"And if we had time for a second book, Ferdinand?"

"I would choose the letter to the Hebrews. You know how the Yala sacrifice animals to all the spirits and idols in order to appease their anger. The writer to the Hebrews admirably demonstrates that the one perfect sacrifice has been offered to the only true God, because Jesus Christ died for our sins once for all. After that, the people will be curious to know who Jesus Christ is, and so we will want to translate Luke and Acts next."

"Amazing, Ferdinand!" Bunkowske exclaimed. "You have seen so many things that I had overlooked. We will translate those four books first, and even if we should be unable to translate any more, we shall have given them enough to lead them to the Savior.'' In 1930 the Yala were about 2 percent Christian. Today they are 33 percent Christian (Bunkowske 1988b, 75-8).

Another example of how cross-cultural ministry broadens our Bible awareness comes from Dr. David Hesselgrave, an Evangelical Free Church missionary who served in Japan. Dr. Hesselgrave suggests an innovative, yet Biblical, manner of dealing with the problem of ancestor worship.

Picture a typical case. A young Japanese man named Hajime moves from a rural village to Tokyo for his university studies. He has no family except his widowed mother, who is his sole means of support. Hajime comes to know Christ during his first year in the university and remains a faithful Christian throughout college. Upon graduation he procures a teaching position at the school in his village. Before Hajime returns home, he stops by to see Hesselgrave, consternation etched on his brow.

''Pastor,'' Hajime begins, ''when I return to my mother's house, I shall be under her authority. She will require me to go with her to the Buddhist and Shinto shrines to worship the spirit of my father. The whole village will expect me to obey my mother and honor the memory of my father, but the Word of God says, 'Worship the Lord your God, and serve him only' (Matt. 4:10). What am I to do?''

Dr. Hesselgrave says that for most of his ministry in Japan, he responded to this question by citing Jesus' words, ''Anyone who loves his father or mother more than me is not worthy of me'' (Matt. 10:37). On the basis of that text, he would urge young Christians like Hajime to choose between their love for their parents and their love for God.

Compared to the Far East, Western culture displays relatively little respect for parents and ancestors. Because of the lack of respect, Western missionaries find it simple to counsel believers, ''Oh, just ignore all that mumbo-jumbo ancestor worship.'' But for Japanese Christians this is a blood-sweat-and-tears choice. Some choose Christ. Others bend under the extreme cultural pressure.

Pondering the tragic results in the latter group, Hesselgrave began to search for another way to counsel people with this common problem. Reading in Luke 16, he found a better way. Here is how he counsels someone like Hajime today.

''Hajime, I can see that you love your Savior, and you also love your mother and the people of your village.''

''Yes, I certainly do.''

''Your problem is that these loves are in conflict. Let us consider how they can be brought into the closest possible agreement. First, let me ask you: Since you love your mother, what would be the best thing that could happen to her?''

''Why, to come to faith in the Lord Jesus, of course,'' Hajime replies. ''Since my conversion, I have prayed every day that the Holy Spirit will work faith in her heart too.''

"Wonderful! Now which course of action will be most helpful in leading her and the town's people to know Christ, your participating in the Buddhist and Shinto rites or your polite but firm refusal?"

"Compromise will not declare the uniqueness of Christ. If I love them, then I must refuse. To fold under the social pressure would be an act of loveless cowardice."

"You have answered well," Hesselgrave affirms. "Let me ask you one more question. How about your ancestors, what would they have you do?"

"What? I don't understand. The dead have not expressed an opinion."

"Yes, they have. Jesus reveals their opinion to us in the story he told about the rich man and Lazarus. Look, in Luke 16 it says, 'The rich man also died and was buried. In hell, where he was in torment, he looked up and saw Abraham far away, with Lazarus by his side. So he called to him, "Father Abraham, have pity on me and send Lazarus to dip the tip of his finger in water and cool my tongue, because I am in agony in this fire' " (Luke 16:22–24). Hajime, even though this is a parable, these are the only words in the whole Bible spoken by a person in hell."

"That makes them especially significant, doesn't it, pastor?"

"Yes. And notice what he says later: 'Send Lazarus to my father's house, for I have five brothers. Let him warn them, so that they will not also come to this place of torment' (Luke 16:27–28). Hajime, according to the words of the dead rich man, what do you think your ancestors would want you to do?"

"Their wish would be that I stand firm in my faith, in order that I might eventually bring the Gospel to the living—my mother and the whole village. Indeed, only in this way can I truly honor the wishes of my ancestors. I see now what I must do. Thank you."

This latter form of counseling is much more likely to be accepted than the former. Rather than pit the love of family against the love of Christ, the two can be united. Rather than imply Hajime's respect for ancestors is unnecessary, his respect is used to motivate proper Christian action (Hesselgrave 1985).

Many similar discoveries of the depth of Biblical teaching are awaiting the person who evangelizes across cultures. It is enlightening to see the features of Holy Scripture that come into focus when we put on the glasses of another culture.

A Real Gospel for a Real World

Many people are fantasy and science fiction fans. To them, escape into an exotic land with bizarre inhabitants is marvelous entertainment. Indeed, some seem to be more concerned about what supposedly happened "long, long ago in a galaxy far, far away" than in the events of their own, real planet. Christians also appreciate this literature. In fact, many classic fantasy stories were created by believers such as George MacDonald, C. S. Lewis, and J.

R. R. Tolkien. Christian writers of this generation are following suit with their own imaginative novels.

What makes for a good fantasy tale? There are at least three key ingredients.

1. The setting must be exotic, totally different from the environment of the reader. The invented worlds must have both extreme beauty and threatening ugliness.

2. There must be an adventure of supreme import that pits good characters against some seemingly invincible evil foe. The weaker the hero, the more the typical reader identifies with him.

3. The heroes must triumph by means of what J. R. R. Tolkien calls "eucatastrophe," literally "good catastrophe." This is the wholly unexpected, yet believable, turn of events which snatches victory from the jaws of defeat. For example, the eucatastrophe of *Cinderella* is that the glass slipper does not change back to its original state. The eucatastrophe of *The Wizard of Oz* is that water melts wicked witches.

By now, you must be wondering what this literary discussion has to do with world evangelization. Everything, because the reality of God's global plan for humankind possesses all the ingredients needed for a great adventure.

1. God is calling you into His world filled with exotic cultures and peoples. All cultures, including your own, display both extreme beauty and the threatening ugliness of human sin. The difference is that the fantasy worlds are only fiction, whereas earth's cultures are real. Indeed, fantasy writers often lift ideas from anthropology books.

2. God is calling you to take part in the adventure of proclaiming Christ to the ends of the earth. He is calling you to be a hero in the battle against Satan and the unbelieving world. Do you feel unequal to the task? Good! In fantasy tales, the weaker the hero, the better. It is the same in God's mission adventure. He assures us, "My grace is sufficient for you, for my power is made perfect in weakness" (2 Cor. 12:9).

3. God is the creator and master of eucatastrophes. J. R. R. Tolkien states this fact in a profound manner:

> The Birth of Christ is the eucatastrophe of Man's history. The Resurrection is the eucatastrophe of the story of the Incarnation. This story begins and ends in joy. . . . There is no tale ever told that men would rather find was true, and none which so many sceptical men have accepted as true on its own merits (Tolkien 1966, 72).

Yes, some folks enjoy escaping into vicarious fantasy adventures. How much more can you and I rejoice in entering and discovering the cultural mosaic of the *real world*?

How much more shall we rejoice in "victory after victory" as He grants us the grace to oppose "the old evil foe"?

How much more shall the joy of salvation be multiplied as men and women around the world come to believe the eucatastrophe that "God was reconciling the world to himself in Christ, not counting men's sins against them. And he has committed to us the message of reconciliation'' (2 Cor. 5:19).

Do Something Now

1. *Search Scripture*. Read Acts 10, 11, and 15. What cultural collisions were occurring in the church at that time? What adjustments did the apostles make to resolve the conflict?

2. *Read*. For a full treatment of cultural differences around the world, read Eugene Nida's *Customs and Cultures*. As intriguing as *Ripley's Believe-It-or-Not*, you will find this book to be eye-opening.

3. *Listen*. Try to establish or improve a friendship with someone of a different culture than yours. "What do I say to them?" most people wonder. The book *Language Acquisition Made Practical* by Tom and Sue Brewster suggests a wealth of conversation starters to help you build relationships.

4. *Look*. If there is a foreign language television channel where you live, turn it on and observe. Jot down what you learn, not just about the language, but also about the culture. If there is no such channel available, go to the art section in your library and look for books that feature art from different countries. Page through some books and jot down what you learn about the culture from their art forms.

5. *Converse*. Obtain a copy of Olgy Gary's *The Luna Game*. As few as ten or as many as 40 can play this simulation game which provides the opportunity to experience the feelings of communicating with a someone of different culture. It will prove a most unique evening's entertainment.

6. *Pray*. Ask yourself if there is a cultural border that you could personally cross. It may be just one person or a whole community. If you live in a monocultural area, look for a cross-environmental border: handicapped, elderly, prison ministry, AIDS victims, and the like. In either case, pray that the Lord would grant you the courage to cross that border and the wisdom to understand and appreciate the mosaic you find there.

Chapter 7

Called to Joy

Saved to Be World Christians

In the movie *The Never Ending Story* a boy named Bastion is given a beautifully bound volume. The book tells of a world called Fantasia, which is being steadily destroyed by a sinister enemy. To find the only person who can save Fantasia, a young hunter is sent on a dangerous quest. Bastion follows the hunter's adventures with great interest, rejoicing with him in his successes and weeping with him in his tragedies. As Bastion arrives at the closing pages, he is dejected and anxious, for the hunter has failed to find the one person who can save them. Only an acre of Fantasia remains, and even that is disintegrating. Then the princess of Fantasia reveals an astonishing secret, "The only one who can save us is the boy who is reading this story."

Feeling as though he has been hit by a lightning bolt, Bastion protests, "She can't mean *me!*"

"Yes, I mean you, Bastion!" shouts the ink on the page before him.

After much convincing and urging, Bastion acknowledges that he is the hero of the book he is reading. Then he performs the deed which is necessary to save Fantasia and return it to its former glory.

Every Christian is in a situation similar to this. We too have read a Book in which we play a key role. When God's Law accuses, it jabs and wounds our hearts. When the Gospel proclaims Christ who gave up His life for sinners, we are the ones compelled by the Holy Spirit personally to trust in this good news. Adult converts especially are aware of what it is like to have believed that the Bible was only a fairy tale and then to be startled into the reality that it *is* reality.

The astonishing realness of the Bible applies not only to our conversion, but also to our discipleship. Christ saved you for a purpose. The Holy Spirit has a quest in which He longs to have you take part. Just as the princess of Fantasia called Bastion's name, so the Lord calls you and all Christians to participate in the adventure of being a world Christian. The aim of this chapter is to discuss what that call entails and how to respond to it.

What Is a World Christian?

What is a world Christian? He or she is a Christian who has set personal priorities in line with God's priorities. To be a Christian but not to live as a world Christian is a contradiction. To be a member of God's family means that one has automatically been called to participate in the Lord's global plans. "A *world* Christian believes that as a prodigal son or daughter, a forgiven sinner who has been graciously accepted as 'family' with the Father and the Son, he cannot honorably separate himself from the family enterprise, which is loving sinners all over the world and calling these hapless children back to their Father" (Board for Communication Services 1986, 13).

World Christians have removed the blinders that kept them from identifying with the needs of the world. They now think, plan, and pray in global terms. World Christians are not content with the status quo, for "inherent in mission is a vital holy impatience, an insatiable reaching out into all those areas which have not yet been penetrated by the Gospel" (Beyerhaus 1971, 18). Nothing is more important to them than that all tribes, tongues, peoples, and nations hear the redeeming Gospel proclaimed in a personal, meaningful manner.

World Christians play two roles. First, there is the role of crossing cultural or environmental barriers to express Christ's love in word and deed. We call such people missionaries. We have reviewed many ways that one can be a missionary both overseas and here at home. The options and opportunities are endless.

The second role is to support world evangelization by informed concern, faithful prayer, and generous giving. We could call such people "commissionaries," because they work with missionaries to fulfill the Great Commission. In fact, the missionaries could hardly function without the support of "commissionaries." There are a hundred ways in which "commissionaries" can aid and promote mission work without ever changing their addresses. Many of these approaches will be outlined in chapter 8.

Christians may play both of these roles to differing degrees. The cross-cultural witness in Vienna or Vietnam is a missionary, but when he prays for another Christian in Quito or Iraq, he is functioning as a "commissionary." The North American "commissionary" who has prayed many years for a Christian friend working in Pakistan may find herself serving as a missionary when a Muslim moves to her block.

A Harmful Misunderstanding

In order to understand better the relationship between the roles of missionary and commissionary, we must recognize a false dichotomy that often occurs in the church. We tend to idolize missionaries, placing them on a pedestal which we do not even care to occupy ourselves.

> It was all or nothing. One was either a full-fledged, full-time career missionary or one was a comfortable, respectable, self-satisfied church member with no *direct, personal* responsibility for the evangelization of the world. If the "call" came, you went; if it didn't, you were free to stay at home and do your own thing. . . .

. . . The people without the "call" were free to go their own way, get good jobs, raise fine families, live in beautiful homes in the luxury and security of suburbia. Those with the "call" were expected to make all the sacrifices while the others were free to enjoy the good things of life bestowed on them by a kind and generous heavenly Father.

This unwarranted, unbiblical dichotomy has been disastrous, both for the cause of missions overseas and for the health and well-being of the church at home (Kane 1986, 205-06).

To avoid this pitfall we need to understand how a missionary differs from other Christians. It is not that missionaries are super saints and all other believers are second rate. The difference is that the missionary has received a special gift from God, the ability to function, and even flourish, in a different culture. In simple terms we could say that this is the ability to live day in and day out in a foreign culture without having a nervous breakdown due to chronic culture shock.

Probably between one and five percent of Christians have this gift. The fact that the gift comes from God frees us from the "up on the pedestal" attitude toward missionaries. Missionaries may not gloat, "*I* am a missionary. Aren't you impressed?" because their ability does not originate from themselves, but from the Creator. Nor does the non-missionary need to feel like a failure or be envious of cross-cultural workers. God is the one who in His wisdom chose not to include the gift of missionary among that individual's particular set of spiritual gifts and abilities (Wagner 1983, 63).

Here is what they have in common. They are all called to serve God wherever they are. We call this concept the *priesthood of all believers*. It means that no matter what you do for a living, it is a holy calling that can be done for the glory of God. "All are called to a life of dedicated Christian service. 'Full-time Christian service' should be a description of every Christian's career" (Sease and Voehringer 1963, 124).

In practical terms, this means that if you work in a factory or an office, you are God's ambassador to that place of business. If you are a checkout clerk at Zayre's, God has called you to that role just as surely as He has called the missionary who serves in Zaire. God knows our strengths and weaknesses. He has given us our gifts and abilities, and He empowers us to serve Him faithfully, no matter where we are. This understanding of the priesthood of all believers removes the smoke screen dichotomy between missionaries and other Christians. We are all called by God. We are all called to sacrifice in order that "the nations [may] be glad and sing for joy" (Ps. 67:4). None of us needs a special gift to serve as a "commissionary" all we need is the desire to obey Him who gave the Great Commission, and then ask Him to show us the one-person-sized job He wants us to tackle.

What Would God Have Me Do?

One of the great missionaries to China, Hudson Taylor, was once requested to speak at a church near London. He agreed, with one stipulation: no offering was to be received. In his message that night Taylor described the vast size, population, and spiritual need of China, and many people were deeply impressed. At the close of the meeting, the leader insisted that Hudson Taylor allow those who were moved to give to his work, but the missionary held his ground. About that decision, Taylor later remarked

> My desire was not that those present might be relieved by giving then and there such contributions as might be convenient under the influence of present emotion, but that each one should go home really burdened with a sense of China's deep need, and then ask God what He would have them do. . . . [P]erhaps in many cases what God was asking was not a money contribution, but personal consecration to His service abroad, or the gift of a dear son or daughter, more precious than gold.
>
> I added that I thought the tendency to take a collection was to leave upon the mind the impression that the all-important thing was money, whereas no amount of money could convert a single soul. The supreme need was that men and women filled with the Holy Spirit should give themselves to the work, and for the support of such there would never be a lack of funds (Murray 1979, 105).

Hudson Taylor's example compels us to face the key issue: What does my Savior require of me in a personal way? I humbly request your permission to discuss this issue in the following pages. I promise I will not twist your arm. Indeed, I cannot change your mind or heart. That is a job for the Holy Spirit; so I'll leave it to Him. All I wish to do is inform your decision. People confronted by God's global plan often entertain doubts, concerns, and questions. This is wholly natural. Let us briefly deal with some possible concerns one by one. Perhaps you will recognize some that are your own.

I Don't Want to Be Motivated by Guilt

Good, I agree! No one should get involved in cross-cultural ministry merely to ease a guilty conscience. To respond to the Great Commission out of shame is a sorry form of discipleship. I have personally known such guilt. Until age 31, I would occasionally toy with the idea of becoming a missionary, mostly to ease my conscience, but nothing ever came of it. Then in October of 1979, the guilt went away, and it has never returned.

What happened? First of all, through a variety of influences, the Holy Spirit led me to assume the joy and duty of being a world Christian. I confessed all my previous blindness to the world's glaring needs, and Christ forgave me. Secondly, the Holy Spirit showed me the me-sized role I could play in world missions. I participated in settling a refugee family. I prayed for and supported my sister-in-law, who was then serving in Japan. Each week I read a little about missions to become informed. And I encouraged my congregation to see the importance of world evangelization. Even though I was only doing a few things, I no longer felt guilty, for I knew that a one-person-sized effort was all that God expected of me.

Remorse may inspire a passing interest, but it cannot endure the obstacles and challenges of serious mission-mindedness. In contrast, gospel-inspired joy, followed by obedience, will lift all sense of mission guilt from your shoulders. The goal of this book has been to motivate you with the joy of salvation, for it alone will result in an enduring commitment to world evangelization.

People Might Think I've Become a Fanatic

There are so many activities at church: the worship services, Sunday school and Bible classes, confirmation, music, youth, young adults, seniors, evangelism, maintenance of the church yard and building, sports teams, the food pantry, the Christmas pageant, and a hundred other things. If an otherwise normal church member suddenly maintains that mission work is the number one activity of the church, are not those involved in other activities going to think that he has gone off the deep end? It is possible.

> Everyone around you—from your boss to your church to your family—will probably do their best to put the chill on your determination to make your life count for the nations. And it's going to seem a lot easier just to become another Jonah (Wilson and Aeschliman n.d., 94).

The major issue is not what people will think of you, but whether or not you are right. After Jesus rose from the dead, He had a one-track mind. There was one subject He constantly emphasized: "Tell My story to the world, to the whole world." Clearly, He had a one-track mind. Putting any other church activity before (or even on a par with) world evangelization is getting off the track. So if some folks accuse you of having a one-track mind, don't worry about it, because you are on the right track.

I Don't Think I Have What It Takes

God is not looking for super heroes. He does not choose only "the best" to participate in world missions like kids choosing sides for basketball. If you are willing to serve Him, He will not leave you waving your hand and begging, "Choose me! Oh, choose me!" The Lord wants ordinary people like you and me.

Jesus' disciples had no unusual skills that placed them head and shoulders above the rest in Judea. The only unusual thing they did was agree to be under His tutelage. Even after three years of Fishers-of-Men training, they were not great paragons of faith. Take a look at Matt. 28:17, a verse immediately before the Great Commission: "When they saw him, they worshiped him; but some doubted." Amazing! Among those whom Jesus was sending out to all nations were some who still doubted. So please drive the thought from your mind that Christ can only use people with mountains of faith. He promised us that those with faith only the size of a mustard seed can still move mountains. The issue is not the greatness of your faith, but whether you rest your weak little faith in the great God (Goldsmith 1976, 103). Trusting in Him, we will be taught the lessons we need in order to grow in faith and effectiveness.

God knows our weaknesses and limitations; yet He has chosen us to do His work. If He is willing to use us and work within our limitations, then we should be willing to do so as well. Roger Buck, missionary to Togo, West Africa, encourages world Christians with these words:

> God helps us take baby steps towards the goals that He has in mind for us. He encourages, "Don't worry. Be a toddler. Take those steps. Just follow me, and it will be easy." Little steps become giant leaps, but not before He makes sure you are ready. Don't delay; the time is now. People's lives are being wasted.

Have you ever seen the inky footprint of a newborn baby? Perhaps you have seen your own among your birth records. Since then, you have done a lot of growing, and the Lord cared for you each step of the way. Similarly, you may be only a newborn or a toddler world Christian right now, but the Spirit will cause you to grow and mature (Eschenbrenner 1987, 2). In a few years the world Christian "will enlarge his knowledge of missions at home and overseas until he can teach a Sunday-school class with at least as much expertise as that of a missionary on furlough. He will also be a welcome resource person on the mission committee of his local church. And certainly he will be a joy to the heart of his pastor" (Kane 1986, 160). God is faithful. He will provide you with what it takes to be a world Christian.

I Hate to Start Something I Might Not Finish

No one likes to be a flash in the pan. How easy it is for us to be hot and excited about something today, only to become lethargic about it tomorrow. How do we keep from falling off the bandwagon, once we have climbed aboard? How do we maintain the interest?

The best place for a world Christian to grow is in a small group of like-minded people. Seek out other believers who have a heart for missions and meet with them regularly. If you know no one else who shares your vision, organize a pilot group of Christian friends who have the potential for becoming world Christians. Invite them to meet for a trial period of six to eight sessions and spend the time studying this book or some other helpful material. When the experimental stage has ended, determine how many wish to continue meeting regularly as a world-Christian study and action group. They are a study group, for they will be constantly learning about missions. They are an action group, for they will roll up their sleeves and engage in both local and distant mission projects.

The combination of study and action is essential to maintain the group's momentum and sense of purpose. Because it is on the cutting edge of God's mission, a world-Christian group will not become stale and stunted as happens to many Bible study groups.

The joy to be experienced in a world-Christian group is an unparalleled blessing. Evangeline Krause has done the church a great service by recording the history of the world-Christian group which gathers in her home the last Saturday of every month. Folks arrive from 3:30 to 4:30 p.m. Mission news and prayers are shared between 4:30 and 5:30. A potluck dinner and general visiting time follow. Missionary Fellowship, as the group is called, first met in August 1955.

> No "superstars." No dynamic preachers or talented organizers who can bring a group together and get them all fired up. Just some ordinary, honest, caring people who were fired up by the Spirit, and concerned that the gospel of Jesus Christ be preached wherever and whenever possible (Krause 1986, 36).

In its first 30 years of existence, Missionary Fellowship raised more than $1.3 million dollars for missions. Thus the title of Evangeline Krause's chronicle is *The Million-Dollar Living Room*. This is one of the most thrilling, joyful, and practical mission books around today. Read it and you'll catch the vision of what God can do through ordinary Christians.

If you worry about not being able to finish what you start, rest assured that belonging to a world-Christian study and action group will keep you growing in mission.

I Might Have to Witness More Right Here

You have reasoned correctly. We cannot be committed to sharing Christ far off without having a renewed interest in local evangelism. For many Christians, the most feared mission opportunities are not the tribes of Africa or the refugees of America. The mission opportunities which strike terror into our hearts are the couple next door, the pals at the office, the friend on the softball team, or our own relatives. These are the relationships which we realize ought to blossom into opportunities to share our faith, and yet so often we fail.

Our local frustrations with witnessing may cause us to conclude, "If I am ineffective at sharing Christ where there is no cultural barrier, I would only be fooling myself to think I could do any good supporting evangelistic work thousands of miles away." Is this conclusion valid? Not at all. When, by the Spirit's power, you dare to include the whole world in your embrace, love and concern for your own neighbors will increase. As you become involved in the lives of people far off, the reports of their repentence and faith will encourage you to work more diligently with those nearby who seem so stiff-necked. As you share the Gospel with foreign neighbors, who perhaps have never heard it before, you will be moved to persevere in prayer for those of your culture, who have already shrugged off the message of salvation.

I Might Have to Change My Lifestyle

This is very possible. Let's consider what might be in store for you. How much time do you spend on forms of entertainment that have no lasting significance? Your priorities will change as you learn to enjoy spending time in study of the world and in prayer for the church around the globe. How many foreigners have you invited to your home in the last year? When you are a world-Christian host, your guest list will become more international. How many missionaries do you know? Before long, you will sense a strong unity with several, as you read their newsletters and meet them personally when they are on furlough. How much of your income do you set aside for investment in God's global enterprise? As your vision expands, so will your "mission stock portfolio" of ministries which you consider it a joy to support.

Materialistic North America does not promote such a lifestyle. We live for the American Dream: "Be free, be in charge, have lots of money, surround yourself with 'good' things, put distance between yourself and the needy. As a culture, we pursue it with a passion" (Wilson and Aeschliman n.d., 102). Financial brokers are the prophets people listen to: "Get a piece of the rock!" "Know no boundaries!" But our broker is Jesus of Nazareth, and when Jesus of Nazareth talks, people ought to listen. He says, "The pagans run after all these things, and your heavenly Father knows that you need them. But seek first his kingdom and his righteousness, and all these things will be given to you as well" (Matt. 6:32-33).

Never has a culture had more things to run after than ours. Every new catalog portrays more gadgets which, if they were bought, would leave our personal mission budget depleted. But there is nothing better in which to invest our money and our lives than the kingdom of God. The profits are guaranteed. "I tell you the truth," our Broker assures, "no one who has left home or brothers or sisters or mother or father or children or fields for me and the gospel will fail to receive a hundred times as much in this present age . . . and in the age to come, eternal life" (Mark 10:29–30).

A hundred times as much. That is 10,000 percent profit. There is a myth that missionaries and their supporters get shortchanged; they give and sacrifice and never have anything to show for it. However, the myth is a lie. Being a world Christian pays a 10,000 percent profit. The dividends are the precious men, women, and children who are bought back from hell by the blood of Christ (Fenton 1973, 101–02).

A fellow who reaped these profits is Steve Burke, who served as a Volunteer Youth Minister in Taiwan. In order to learn the language and culture, he lived for five months with an upper-class Chinese family. Mr. Huang was the president of the Taiwan branch of a New York insurance agency. Mrs. Huang was a homemaker. From the viewpoint of Steve's hosts, living in North America would have been like dying and going to heaven. So they could not fathom why he had come to Asia to work as a volunteer. Their questions about his motives opened the door for him to share with them about Christ and the eternal riches of God's grace. Eventually the Holy Spirit used

118

Steve's witness to convince Mrs. Huang that Christ had paid the price for her liberation. She was baptized and began to tell friends and neighbors about the joy and peace she has in Jesus, possessions which all the money in the world cannot buy.

Mrs. Huang is proof that we receive back a hundred times what we invest. Steve Burke knows that any change in his lifestyle was worth the joyous dividend of seeing a precious human being saved. And the same is true for all the "commissionaries" back home who were supporting Steve. The time they invested in prayer for his ministry was compensated a hundredfold. The funds they contributed to cover his expenses were the wisest investment they ever made.

Yes, being a world Christian will alter your lifestyle, but it will never cramp your lifestyle. It is not a sacrifice, but the highest privilege.

What If the Mission Work I Support Fails?

Some Christians have caught the disease of mission pessimism, for they assume that mission work is always strenuous labor with little fruit to show for it. This is true in some areas where missionaries have preached for decades before the angels could rejoice over one sinner who repented. Courageous, persistent world Christians are needed to support challenging ministries such as Muslim and Hindu work. However, we ought not conclude that all mission work is showing meager results. The Holy Spirit is working wonders around the globe. Among many peoples the company of the redeemed is growing much more rapidly than it is in your community.

Nevertheless, it cannot be denied that at times the going will be rough. The work may flounder. The missionaries you support may be disappointed. You may feel like quitting. What will you do then? Episcopalian missionary Elisabeth Elliot provides thoughtful advice in her little book *These Strange Ashes*, which relates her first attempts at mission work among the Colorado Indians of Ecuador. After a year of strenuous labor, everything that could go wrong did go wrong, with disastrous results. As the reader approaches the last page of this story, he expects a surprise happy ending, but it does not appear. Instead, Elisabeth Elliot concludes that God had allowed her to sacrifice (according to human standards, waste) a year of her life for some reason known only to Him. The book ends with a little parable for all those who worry about possible failure:

> A story is told of Jesus and His disciples walking one day along a stony road. Jesus asked each of them to choose a stone to carry for Him. John, it is said, chose a large one while Peter chose the smallest. Jesus led them then to the top of a mountain and commanded that the stones be made bread. Each disciple, by this time tired and hungry, was allowed to eat the bread he held in his hand, but of course Peter's was not sufficient to satisfy his hunger. John gave him some of his.
>
> Some time later Jesus again asked the disciples to pick up a stone to

119

carry. This time Peter chose the largest of all. Taking them to the river, Jesus told them to cast the stones into the water. They did so, but looked at one another in bewilderment.

"For whom," asked Jesus, "did you carry the stone?" (Elliot 1975, 132).

I Am Afraid of the Unknown

Often people avoid any involvement in Christian missions for fear that they might get stuck with more than they bargained for. "If I start helping drug addicts, God might trap me in such work full-time. Or, if I befriend international students, He might inspire me to become a missionary in another country. Why, God only knows what might happen to me!"

Isn't that the very point? We don't know what the future holds, but our loving Lord does. The Holy Spirit never sends anyone anywhere without preparing him or her in some way. The Father never sends anyone anywhere that He is not already present. Christ never asks us to love people that He does not already love.

The question is not "Can God be trusted?" The question is "Will we trust God with our lives?"

Come, Join the Adventure!

Hudson Taylor refused to take an offering because he preferred that people give themselves before they gave anything else. This is also what Paul, the first great missionary, encourages you to give: "I urge you, brothers, in view of God's mercy, to offer your bodies as living sacrifices, holy and pleasing to God—this is your spiritual act of worship" (Rom. 12:1). Missionary to Thailand Dennis Denow speaks of his encounter with the will of God as stated in this Bible verse:

> Over twelve years ago, I was reading this verse when it struck me that I had never done what it says. I had never offered my body to God as a living sacrifice for Him to use. I had been serving in Lutheran high schools for about eight years, and I could see God's blessing on my ministry. But, at that moment, it seemed extremely important for me to perform this "spiritual act of worship."
>
> I put down my Bible and told the Lord that I was offering Him my body for His use. I would go where He wanted and do what He wanted me to do. He could change me in any way He desired. There were no lightning bolts or angel choruses, but from that time things began to change. My ministry began to change. I began to change.
>
> For me the important thing about this verse is the conscious decision to turn control over to God. I no longer worry if I'm in the right place doing the right thing. When discouragements hit, I'm reminded that my body and my life are His, and He doesn't make mistakes. I am confident of God's

blessing, because I know that I am where He wants me to be.

Dennis learned to trust God with his life, both at home during the years he worked as a "commissionary" and now in Thailand working as a missionary. You and I can do the same.

The princess of Fantasia called to Bastion to rescue her realm, and Bastion questioned, "Who, me?" The Almighty God calls you and me to be Christians who share His global compassion. And how shall we respond? God's desire to include us in the world evangelization process was not an afterthought on His part. Ever since the Fall, He intended to call us into the adventure! How do we know that? Look at what Luke records from the evening of the first Easter:

> Then he opened their minds so they could understand the Scriptures. He told them, "This is what is written: The Christ will suffer and rise from the dead on the third day, and repentance and forgiveness of sins will be preached in his name to all nations, beginning at Jerusalem" (Luke 24:45-47).

Jesus refers to two kinds of prophecies. First, there are the messianic prophecies which foretold the events of His life, especially His suffering and rising from the dead. We cherish these prophecies, for they are living miracles which validate the veracity of the Gospel story. But the second category of prophecies we often overlook. "Repentance and forgiveness of sins will be preached in his name to all nations" (Luke 24:47). The worldwide proclamation of the Gospel was foretold by the prophets (see Micah 4:1–5; Ps. 87; and Zech. 8:20–23). Grasp what this means. When you pray for a missionary or national Christian in another hemisphere, you are fulfilling the prophecy that repentance and forgiveness of sins would be preached in that place. When you make the effort to befriend the neighbor who does not know the name of Christ, you are fulfilling prophecy. Therefore, the world Christian stands in the very center of God's will.

What a thrill to be part of the fulfillment of God's prophecy! What an honor to participate in God's centuries-long enterprise of proclaiming His mighty acts to the nations! What a joy to be part of the adventure of world evangelization!

> Sing to the Lord, for he has done glorious things; let this be known to all the world. Shout aloud and sing for joy, people of Zion, for great is the Holy One of Israel among you (Is. 12:5–6).

Don't miss out on the joy, my friend. This is what you were made for. This is the *cause* worth living for. This is what Christ saved you for. So what are you saving yourself for? Come! Trusting in the power of the Holy Spirit, let us embrace the adventure and run the race together.

Do Something Now

1. *Search Scripture*. Compare Matt. 9:37–38 and Rev. 7:9–10. Make a list of the things that must occur before the Revelation text will become a reality.

2. *Read*. You will enjoy Paul Little's fantastic booklet *Affirming the Will of God*. The insights found in these few pages will help you determine what God wants you to do to help fulfill the Great Commission.

3. *Listen*. Look up your favorite mission hymns and give them a good sing. As you vocalize and ponder the words, thank the Lord that the joy of sharing Christ cross-culturally is not reserved for missionaries only, but is for all world Christians.

4. *Look*. The book *The Hidden Half* by Sam Wilson and Gordon Aeschliman is good reading, but the art on the cover is a lesson in itself. In a quiet place, away from any disturbances, study that picture in detail. Imagine that you are the various people portrayed.

5. *Converse*. Talk with other Christians about starting a world-Christian study and action group. If people seem hesitant, begin with a three-month trial period. Do not be discouraged if only one person responds. Praising God for that one mission partner, go ahead and meet together regularly.

6. *Pray*. Meditate on Rom. 12:1–2. Do not overlook the context; Paul has just spent three chapters discussing God's plan to save both Jews and Gentiles. What is the motive for giving your body as a living sacrifice? Ask God to reveal to you in the coming days and years ways that you might offer yourself to Him.

Chapter 8
Multiplying the Joy

The Mission Role of the Local Church

Office supplies were running low at Our Savior Lutheran. Knowing that a new set of letterhead stationery and envelopes must soon be printed, the pastor had asked an artist in the congregation to design a logo for the church. Now the pastor was presenting the artist's work to the board of elders to receive their approval. "Here is what I propose as the logo for Our Savior," he said, unveiling a drawing of the church's steeple against a backdrop of the world.

The elders studied the logo with quizzical looks on their faces. Eventually, a couple of them muttered, "It's certainly drawn quite well," but otherwise they were not enthusiastic. Taken aback by their lackluster reaction, the pastor questioned, "All right, fellows, what is it that you don't like?"

Finally, one of them put their apprehensions into words, "It isn't that we don't like it, Pastor. It just seems inappropriate."

"Inappropriate?"

"Yes. After all, what does Our Savior have to do with the world?"

Those elders, and all Christians, need "to grasp how wide and long and high and deep is the love of Christ" (Eph. 3:18). While God desires that every congregation recognize His worldwide purposes, the people of God often have trouble seeing beyond the city limits. Some assume that by becoming a Christian they have done nothing more than take out membership in an ecclesiastical club, when in reality God has enlisted them in a military campaign to free people from the oppression of sin, death, and the devil.

> As it is, most of the churches in the Western world are self-centered, inward-looking, preaching self-denial but all the while practicing self-indulgence. They are preoccupied with their own problems and concerned almost exclusively for their own growth. They are playing at missions (Kane 1986, 205).

The first goal of this book is to awaken Christian readers to the joy of being a world Christian. The second goal is to have world Christians lead their churches to become world congregations, producing waves of mission action which will break on earth's most distant shores. This second step is absolutely necessary, because the local Christian church is the center of Christian mission endeavor.

"*My* church is the center?" you may ask. That's right! Not the mission

123

board headquarters. Not the distant mission fields. Your church, and my church, and all Christian congregations are the center of the mission enterprise.

> As a womb for the nurture of future missionaries, the local church is potentially unexcelled. What does or does not happen at that level profoundly and gravely affects what can or cannot be done at any other level (Winter 1978, 20).

The womb of missionaries! That is the local congregation. It is the womb, because every missionary grows up in a congregation. Potential missionaries populate your church right now: the toddler swinging his feet in the pew, the teenage girl teaching vacation Bible school, the man working on his M.B.A. degree, the widow with several healthy years before her. They could serve in a cross-cultural or cross-environmental role somewhere in the world if their church nurtured them and encouraged them to follow as the Holy Spirit leads and directs them. Similarly, every "commissionary" belongs to a local congregation. There he/she is nourished on the Word of God. There he/she works to involve others in God's global cause.

Therefore, the purpose of this final chapter is to outline how you can multiply your mission joy so that your local family of Christians will live up to its role as the center of missions and the womb of missionaries.

The Mission Role of the Pastor

Sometimes mission reluctance in the parish comes from a most unexpected quarter—the pastor. Usually this is not the case, for ministers have dedicated their lives to proclaiming the good news of Jesus Christ. However, where clergy opposition does occur, it is a formidable roadblock that must be removed. The question is how. The strategy will depend on the reason for the minister's reluctance.

1. Some pastors are simply unaware of the key roles that they and their churches play in world evangelization. If this seems to be the problem, ask your pastor to read this book or some other text that will reveal to him his responsibility. A good example is Andrew Murray's classic *Key to the Missionary Problem*. Murray (1828-1917), a Dutch Reformed clergyman from South Africa, makes observations which will give you and your pastor plenty to discuss:

> It is one thing for a minister to be an advocate and supporter of missions: it is another and very different thing for him to understand that missions are the chief end of the church, and therefore the chief end for which *his congregation* exists. It is only when this truth masters him in its spiritual power, that he will be able to give the subject of missions its true place in his ministry. . . . He must learn how to lead the congregation on to make the extension of Christ's kingdom the highest object of its corporate existence (Murray 1979, 18).

Another approach would be to talk to your pastor about other ministers who have the understanding of the local congregation that Murray describes. For example, the November 1987 *Lutheran Witness* carried an article entitled "Where Missions Are Everybody's Business," describing the mission commitment of Pastor Charles Roluffs and Pastor Mark Bertermann at Beautiful Savior Lutheran Church in Milwaukie, Oregon (Buth 1987, 8-9).

2. Busy pastors may feel that they do not have sufficient time in their crowded schedules to give world evangelization the stress that they know it deserves. Perhaps they have been scolded by parishioners: "You had better attend to your local responsibilities rather than focus attention on distant mission work!" Harsh warnings of this sort may have tarnished your minister's original idealism about the Great Commission. But below the tarnish there is still silver. All he needs is your support. Let him know that you share his concern for evangelism and cross-cultural outreach. Volunteer your time and energies to promote world evangelization in your church.

3. Mission-related guilt, frustration, and fears may explain the pastor's reluctance to emphasize mission work in his parish. Some pastors place missionaries on a pedestal just as much as lay people do. When a missionary comes to speak at his church, he may feel guilty and chide himself, "I should be a missionary, but I lack the commitment."

The pastor, like lay people, needs to find his own one-person-sized role. He needs to recognize that some are called by God to work cross-culturally and others are not. If he has the gift of being able to work cross-culturally, he may find fulfillment serving as a missionary in some local ethnic ministry without ever having to move to a distant mission field. If he does not have this gift, he can help fulfill the Great Commission by faithfully challenging himself and his parishioners to live as world Christians.

No matter what the cause of the pastor's reluctance, remember to deal with him pastorally. Challenge him with God's commands, but be patient with him. Give him time to deal with the facts that you present to him. Pray for him. Encourage him with the message of salvation by grace through faith in Christ, just as he has encouraged you many times. With such pastoral care, your minister will become a world pastor, so that together you can work to make your church a world congregation.

The Role of the Mission Committee

Usually the most efficient way to promote mission awareness in the congregation is through the formation of a mission committee. The main objectives of the committee are (1) to integrate mission education into the total church program; (2) to encourage God's people to devote their time, abilities, and financial resources to God's global purposes; and (3) to sensitize, motivate, and guide the congregation to participate in cross-cultural ministry opportunities near at hand.

Here are some suggested resources:

First, get in touch with the mission board of your denomination. Ask for materials about how to run a mission committee and for basic informational and promotional materials.

Second, materials may also be requested from other mission societies and organizations that interest your group.

Third, David Bryant provides many fine suggestions in chapters 15–17 of his book *In the Gap*.

Fourth, The Association of Church Missions Committees (ACMC) provides training conferences, helpful literature, and consulting services for the local church mission committee. The address of ACMC is P.O. Box ACMC, Wheaton, IL 60187 or 1620 S. Myrtle Ave., Monrovia, CA 91016.

Fifth, the Great Commission Resource Library at Concordia Theological Seminary in Fort Wayne, Indiana, has available for purchase Morris Watkins' *Missions Resource Handbook*. This book contains many helpful ideas and resources for promoting missions in the local church. A mission committee that makes use of any of these resources will be on good footing.

To start with, you want to make world evangelization the unifying purpose of your church. Also, you need to make mission outreach as people-centered as possible. Then, having accomplished these goals, you can expect people from your own fellowship to go out as missionaries. The remainder of this chapter develops these three key goals.

Make World Evangelization the Unifying Purpose

So much is happening in the local parish that it is sometimes difficult to remember what the central purpose of the church is. "Whoever turns a sinner from the error of his way will save him from death and cover over a multitude of sins" (James 5:20). People are perishing. The local church exists that they shall not perish. Worship services, Sunday school, choir practices, Bible studies, youth group meetings, singles outings, shut-in calling, and every other parish activity occur because God sent His Son to rescue the perishing. God sent Him to the whole world, because He loves everyone from every place and every culture.

Yet so often churches turn inward. They live as though God loved only them. They think, plan, and spend their resources as though Christ had died for them alone. Narrowness and self-interest deafen their ears to the call of Christ, "As the Father has sent me, I am sending you" (John 20:21). They overlook the Great Commission as though no one were perishing beyond their walls.

This predicament indicates that the primary work of the mission committee must be to convince their brothers and sisters in the faith that missions is the unifying cause and purpose for all that they do. Let us investigate some ways this can be accomplished.

Demonstrate that Mission Outreach Is Biblical

Many Christians view world evangelization as a minor theme of Scripture. Is it? Every book of the New Testament was written by a missionary. The only authoritative history of the early church, the book of Acts, is a missionary journal. The disciples were first called Christians in a foreign, missionary church (Acts 11:19–26). Every epistle in the New Testament written to a church was written to a foreign mission church. Of the twelve apostles chosen by Christ all but one became missionaries; the only one who did not became a traitor (Polack 1930, 11–12). As you share such facts, folks will eventually recognize that God's global cause is the major theme of their Bibles.

Encourage mission-related Bible reading. An eye-opening activity is to read the Bible and underline in red all the passages which talk about God's concern for the nations. Try it. Your eyes will be opened. Words like *peoples, nations, the world,* and *everyone* will begin to catch your attention. Names and places will take on new meaning. Consider the man who carried Jesus' cross, Simon of Cyrene. Where is Cyrene? When you find out, you will see the international significance of his role in the Good Friday drama. People and stories that you took for granted before will now be viewed from a global perspective. For example, you will have to mark the whole book of Ruth in red, because it is the tale of a foreign woman who left her idols so that her mother-in-law's God could be her God. Do not be surprised if your Bible turns almost half red, because all the world is in all the Word (Bryant 1985, 81). Let the red ink remind you of how Christ's heart bled for all the world.

Demonstrate that Mission Outreach Is Lutheran

Some people want to know whether Luther and other early Lutherans encouraged taking the Gospel to foreign lands. Perhaps the most well-known mission quotation comes from Luther's *Large Catechism* in his explanation of the petition "Thy kingdom come." This we pray "both in order that we who have accepted it may remain faithful and grow daily in it and in order that it may gain recognition and followers among other people and advance with power throughout the world" (Tappert 1959, 427). Unfortunately, direct references to world evangelization do not abound in the Lutheran Confessions. Nevertheless, they emphasize salvation by grace through faith. That message is for all the world. The Gospel is global in scope. Therefore the concern and ministry of Lutherans—and all Christians—must be global as well.

For a detailed portrayal of Martin Luther's commitment to mission outreach, read Eugene Bunkowske's article "Was Luther a Missionary?" in the April–July 1985 *Concordia Theological Quarterly.* Or try chapter two of James Scherer's book *Gospel, Church, and Kingdom.* There is another reason that we can say with confidence that world evangelization is Lutheran: Luther is still a missionary. His boldness in proclaiming salvation by Christ's grace alone is still leading people around the world to find comfort in this marvelous good news.

Demetrio, a high school student of Manila, was interested in the study of history. One day he came upon the story of Martin Luther, who was bold to preach the Gospel though the forces of his day opposed him. Demetrio read every scrap of information he could find on Luther in the libraries of his city. Then he announced to his family that he was a Lutheran. But where was the Lutheran Church?

He searched for it all through Manila. Nobody knew of a single Lutheran church in the city and its environs. After years of waiting, Demetrio heard the report that a Lutheran mission had been established in a suburb. He searched for and found it (Dorn 1962, 56).

Do not assume that Demetrio's story is an isolated case. In Caracas, Venezuela, Douglas Prada read about Luther in his high school history class and admired Luther's courage. However, since there was no Lutheran church in his part of the city, Douglas assumed there was none to be found. Several months later, he heard about *El Salvador Lutheran Church* in another part of the city. The next Sunday morning Douglas was there to find out what Lutheranism was all about. Four members of the congregation sat down with him after the service, and for the next two hours they shared Law and Gospel with Douglas. He left having discovered the grace of God in Jesus his Savior.

Is mission outreach part of the Lutheran heritage? Ask Demetrio and Douglas.

World Mission and Christian Education

When does the recruitment and training of world Christians begin? It must begin as early as all other Christian instruction. Teachers can convey God's worldwide concern even to the youngest of children because most Bible stories are a door to talking about the mission God has given us. Start with Genesis 1 and 2. The doctrine of creation presupposes that God is the Lord of all the earth, of all mankind, of all peoples.

Morris Watkins has provided Christian educational agencies with two wonderful tools. *The Great Commission Study Guide* is a brief, question-and-answer resource for teaching the significance of the Great Commission to youth and adult confirmation classes. It deserves to be included as "the seventh chief part of the catechism." *Seven Worlds to Win* is a detailed treatment of the major regions of the world from the perspective of religion, providing information that rarely appears in secular textbooks. With *Seven Worlds to Win* a Christian social studies teacher can give children a heart for the world.

Another good idea is to form children's mission clubs. Organized somewhat like the scouting program, mission clubs inform, involve, and inspire children with regard to cross-cultural ministry. The Southern Baptist Conference and other churches use such clubs very effectively. In them, children learn to give world evangelization top priority at an early age—an idea well worth imitating.

When does the recruitment and training of world Christians end? Never. The pastor and the mission committee will devise means for adolescent and adult believers to continually grow in mission.

World Mission and Worship

In one congregation a survey was taken to discover the members' opinions regarding the minister's sermons. Several people filed the complaint that too many sermons included references to personal witnessing and missions. Instead, they wanted to hear messages on topics that concerned them. These folks failed to comprehend that witnessing and missions *are* their concern, because God has appointed them their brothers' keepers. Preachers will do well to keep this major concern before their flock.

Even if pastors were to leave world evangelization out of their sermons, it would still sound loud and clear in traditional Lutheran liturgies. In 1663, during an era when many Lutherans were lackadaisical towards proclaming God's Word to other lands, Baron Justinian von Weltz, an Austrian nobleman, issued a number of tracts in favor of mission outreach. To defend his position, von Weltz called attention to the parts of the liturgy which expressed God's universal love for mankind (Polack 1930, 54–55). The liturgies of our day still emphasize this theme, though we may overlook it. Sit down with the liturgy you commonly use and read it as though you had never heard it before. You will find several phrases and sections that refer to God's worldwide plan of salvation. In order to help others take note of the mission references in the liturgy, you could have a special service in which these sections are highlighted in some way, perhaps by a note sounded on a trumpet, or by printing them in the bulletin.

Our hymnals feature mission sections and there are perhaps 30 other hymns which have a strong mission emphasis. Other than that, however, our hymns display some glaring weaknesses. One weakness is vagueness. Sometimes an outreach theme is hidden in symbolic language. A case in point is the classic "Onward, Christian Soldiers." Onward to where? What are we fighting about? How do we fight? How do we win? Reread the words of this hymn and you will not find a clear answer to any of these questions.

Another weakness in our hymns is the overabundance of self-centered texts. In many hymns that speak of the Christian life, the main encouragement is to lead a life free from sin or to remain steadfast in the faith so that we can get to heaven while saying nothing about spreading the Gospel. Evangelical missiologist Ralph Winter laments:

> In our hymn books there is no balance. In our Bible studies there is no balance. In our sermons there is no balance. In the Christian bookstores there is no balance. All . . . our mining of the gold in the Bible emphasizes for us the blessings that we are to receive [and] minimizes the blessings

others are to receive from us (Winter 1982, tape 1, side a).

Clearly, what the church needs is a troop of new hymn writers to make necessary revisions in our present hymns and to write new songs which will sound the call of the Great Commission in fresh ways. Perhaps someone in your congregation has this gift. Why not compose hymns that go into some detail about sharing Christ in a specific country or region of the world? Why not write a hymn about reaching Hindus or Jews or Muslims or Mormons or adherents of the New Age religions? Why not hymns that deal with modern themes like urban ministry, North American ethnic opportunities, Bible translation, or media outreach? No doubt, some able Christians have already penned lines on some of these subjects. More needs to be written. More needs to be shared with sister congregations. Let us sing new songs to the Lord of the harvest.

Frequently, the prayers offered during public worship do not reach beyond the needs of the congregation. We pray: "Aunt Mildred is due for surgery on Tuesday; grant her Your healing, Lord. Ed Walker is out of work; open doors for him. John and Linda will be united in holy matrimony next Friday; bless their life together. The youth group is traveling to a regional gathering; keep them safe and build their faith." These concerns certainly merit our prayerful attention, but they should be accompanied by petitions which demonstrate that our gathering of believers is but one local chapter of an international organization with global interests and responsibilities. When we pray about world concerns, we follow the counsel of missionary Paul, who urged Christians to pray for all the saints (Eph. 6:18) and for everyone (1 Tim. 2:1).

Another way to stress missions in our corporate worship is to let the diversity of worship forms in other lands enrich our worship. During a service that includes the Sacrament of Baptism, show the movie *Salifu's Harvest*, which includes footage from a mass baptism in Ghana, West Africa. The joy of the African worshipers will overflow into your congregation that Sunday.

Our celebration of the Lord's Supper can be heightened by cross-cultural insights. In Ghana the intimacy of sharing food is very important. To eat together is to declare mutual peace and friendship. This understanding sheds light on Paul's words: "Because there is one loaf, we, who are many, are one body, for we all partake of the one loaf " (1 Cor. 10:17).

In many countries converts are ostracized by their families. The convert then needs a new sense of family. Being with fellow believers fills this need. However, in cultures where ancestors are highly honored, the convert also asks, "Do I have ancestors now?" The answer is that the Christians of past ages are his ancestors. Thus, liturgical phrases such as "with all the company of heaven" are especially meaningful to him. Sharing this story with a North American congregation can help make the phrase more meaningful to them as well.

Doris Engstrom, missionary to Nigeria, West Africa, reflects on the Nigerian style of receiving the offering:

The choir moves up the aisle to a table before the altar. And then, row by row, one by one, every person in the church follows.

But they don't just go up to the front. They go forward with joy and a real feeling of thanksgiving. They sing and clap and even dance. It is not just a time to give money. It is a time to give the Lord all that is His, including our very selves. It's a time to recommit yourself to His purpose. It is done with joy—total joy.

How different than sitting in the pew and passing a plate. If one is daydreaming, the offering can be easily ignored.

I wonder if it isn't possible for money to pass from checkbooks to the church treasury without ever going through hearts. I wonder if we truly think of it as a response to His Word (Engstrom and Engstrom 1986, 2).

Perhaps your congregation would benefit from a North American adaptation of the Nigerian offering.

The above examples indicate ways that a pastor or mission committee can make world evangelization a regular part of congregational worship. The story of the Nigerian offering, however, brings us to another crucial topic which many people call "the bottom line."

The Church's Mission and Stewardship

The mission committee will not have attained its goal of making world evangelization the church's central focus until it wins the battle of the budget. When the voters assembly finds itself in the red, which budget item is most likely to be cut? Often it is missions.

The kingdom of God cannot expand when God's people slash the kingdom-work budget. For example, the 1969 mission budget of the Lutheran Church-Missouri Synod was 11 million dollars. Twenty years later, the mission budget is just about the same. Considering inflation, congregations are actually dedicating fewer funds to reach the ends of the earth than they did in 1969. And considering the increase in the income of churchgoers over the last two decades, we can conclude that greater affluence does not necessarily lead to greater generosity.

Perhaps we need to learn a lesson from Papua New Guinea. After Westerners entered that land, the Papuans sought the answer to an intriguing question:

How does it come about that the white man is so astonishingly rich, when he is not seen to work particularly hard? His ships go on and on bringing him goods without measure. His aircraft deliver these goods to the individual white man. Machines arrive complete and ready for use. The white man is never seen to pay for these things: apparently he gets them all free. They are sent out from inexhaustible storehouses, which belong to a higher power (Vicedom 1961, 59).

This thinking, which seemed very logical to the Papuans, resulted in the formation of new religions called cargo cults. Adherents of these groups sought to discover the secret by which the white men gained access to the higher power's inexhaustible storehouses. Some cargo cults sought wealth by trying to copy the Westerners in every detail, hoping that this would please the Western God. Others used elements of their pagan religions, such as employing magic rituals to make money appear out of thin air and calling upon the ancestors to help them fulfill their desires. No matter what the method used, the goal was always the same: to compel God to open the windows of heaven and pour out upon them airplanes filled with modern blessings. Many Papuans who had earlier confessed Christ as Lord were led astray by the materialistic appeal of the cargo cults.

Now we might laugh at the foolishness of the cargo cults, but is the Western church really any wiser? In our own way, many North Americans are adherents of the cargo cult. The Papuans only dream about wealth and luxury. We have them! We strive and sweat to have more. Sure, we work hard for what we own; it doesn't fall out of the sky as some Papuans think. But the problem is that we never seem to be satisfied. Couldn't it be said that we worship the cargo, too? In Papua New Guinea it is called a cargo cult. In North America it is called materialism. In both cases, it is idolatry.

We say we trust God to save us eternally, but do we trust Him to save us financially? If we did, then our giving to mission work would not be so paltry. The average annual giving of North American Christians to overseas mission work is about 15 dollars. No wonder the Scriptures must compel us, " 'Bring the whole tithe. . . . Test me in this,' says the Lord Almighty, 'and see if I will not throw open the floodgates of heaven and pour out so much blessing that you will not have room enough for it' " (Mal. 3:10). This is the command and promise of the Lord of wallets and budgets.

How can you lead your congregation to tremble at this Word and obey? By constantly placing world evangelization, both near and distant, at the center of your church's budget. In all stewardship drives and financial reports, demonstrate that expanding the kingdom of Christ is the goal behind all the expenses. A key way to do this is to emphasize people over programs. We need to emphasize especially the people who are being called out of darkness into God's marvelous light. Here is an example.

Dr. Alvin Barry, a district president of the LCMS, was once in India visiting churches. In the town of Krishnagiri, Pastor Devasagayam posed a question to Doctor Barry. "Do you know how many years the first missionary preached here before he had one convert?"

"How long?"

"Twenty years," was the reply. "And I was that first convert!" Pastor Devasagayam announced with a grin.

"Praise God!"

"Do you have any idea how much money your church expended so that one person—myself—could be converted to faith in Christ?"

Caught off guard by the question, Doctor Barry simply shook his head.

"It cost over $100,000 dollars to save me, but I was worth it!" the minister declared proudly. "I was worth it, because Christ gave His precious blood, more valuable than any sum of money, to ransom me from death. And I was worth it because I did not hoard what God gave to me. Over the years, the Holy Spirit has so blessed my preaching and personal witnessing that, by the grace of God, hundreds of my people have also become co-heirs of the riches of Christ.''

Pastor Devasagayam is one of the faces behind the figures of your parish budget. When human faces take precedence over figures, the voters will sing a different tune about budget cuts: "Mission work is the last item we can cut! We dare not take a chance that even one missionary might be recalled.''

Personalize Missions

As we have just seen, for mission work to come alive it must be made personal. One way to accomplish this is to truly befriend someone who is working on the front lines. Far too many churches support missions while failing to support missionaries. That is, they give cold cash to their denominational mission board, but they never develop a warm friendship with any particular missionary. Your mission committee should start by choosing one missionary and then concentrate on fostering a meaningful relationship. The "Together in Mission" program of the Missouri Synod, which links missionaries and congregations, is one attempt at personalizing support. Such programs are beneficial, not only for the congregation, but for the missionary as well. Missionaries are human. They need more than an occasional prayer or monetary gift; they want to be loved.

Become Informed

How do you develop a personal relationship with a missionary? The first rule is to be informed. Those who fail to inform themselves will stick their foot in their mouth, as illustrated by this story:

> "Well, it's wonderful to see you home again," a friend of mine greeted me enthusiastically, when I returned from work in Indonesia for my first furlough. "You must tell us all about your work in South America," he continued. I reminded him that we had actually been in Indonesia, and wondered to myself just what effect our letters had produced. "Oh, yes," he replied casually, "I knew it was somewhere out there" (Goldsmith 1976, 117).

To avoid such ignorance, read the newsletters of your chosen missionary faithfully. Study a little bit each month about the place where he serves. In the geography section of your library hunt for books about his country. Do not overlook the children's section of the library. It may have some excellent books or recordings. When you write letters to your missionary, ask him/her questions that reflect what you have been learning. This will encourage the missionary to respond, because he will know that you are taking his work seriously.

Pray Faithfully

Prayer is another means of maintaining a personal relationship. When you promise to pray for a missionary, really do so. Dedicate a prominent spot on your daily prayer list to him, his family, and his work. Don't fall into the trap of thinking that missionaries are such model Christians that they require little prayer support. How easy it is to picture missionaries as Super-Christians, always witnessing, never afraid, always serving others, never tired or lonely or homesick. This is not how the Bible describes them. Paul says, "But we have this treasure in jars of clay to show that this all-surpassing power is from God and not from us" (2 Cor. 4:7). While the Gospel is gloriously powerful, missionaries are not. They are like clay pots, easily chipped, cracked, and shattered. A former missionary's wife tells it like it is:

> Spiritually, my time in the Philippines was a dry desolation. I read the text in the *Portals of Prayer* and called that my Bible study. I still sent prayers like buckshot at sporadic intervals, and concentrated through entire worship services on keeping my children quiet. As missionaries we exhorted these nominally Christian lowland Filipinos to believe the Bible and study it, to trust the Lord to forgive them and trust Him to deliver them through the drought, and I felt like the person with the log in one eye pointing to the person with the speck.

When you draw up your missionary prayer list, include a petition that the missionaries would get along with each other. Several studies have shown that the major reason that missionaries leave the field is abrasive, even antagonistic, relations with other missionaries. This is a problem that exists in all denominations. How Satan must laugh when he sees our army splintered by dissension, strife, and bitterness!

Missionaries are fragile; so handle them with prayer. Most of all, pray that they will be bold to share the Gospel, not yielding to the many pressures against them. Paul often requested such petitions:

> And pray for us, too, that God may open a door for our message, so that we may proclaim the mystery of Christ, for which I am in chains. Pray that I may proclaim it clearly, as I should (Col. 4:3–4).

> Pray also for me, that whenever I open my mouth, words may be given me so that I will fearlessly make known the mystery of the gospel, for which I am an ambassador in chains. Pray that I may declare it fearlessly, as I should (Eph. 6:19–20).

Since Paul needed such intercession, be assured that missionaries today also desire and need prayer support from you and your church.

Take a personal interest in the people to whom the missionary is ministering. When individuals are mentioned in the missionary's newsletter, write their names down and learn them, no matter how foreign they may sound to your ear. Pray for them and keep tabs on their development. If at all possible, get to know people nearby who are from the country where your missionary serves. Your face-to-face contact with them will help you identify with the work overseas and pray more faithfully.

Tim and Beth Heiney, missionaries to Ghana, in West Africa, speak of the encouragement that two national believers, Salifu and Tomabu, received from knowing that Christians far away were praying for them when they faced great difficulties:

> Salifu recently asked Tim if he'd asked everyone to pray for him in the newsletter. Tim said we had, and Salifu grinned. He told us that not only did he get his teaching job back but he was placed in the same village he'd taught in before and didn't need to move his family. Also, his peanut harvest did real well. How exciting to watch this young Christian seeing his God at work!
>
> When talking to Tomabu recently, he was rejoicing in the birth of another child. He was so happy that everything went well because, when his wife went into labor, he said, he didn't do any sacrifices or pray to any idols. He gathered his whole family together and prayed to God for help (Heiney and Heiney 1988, 5).

Does prayer make a difference? Salifu, Tomabu, and the North Americans who prayed for them will affirm that it does. For more instruction on mission-related prayer, read Wesley Duewel's *Touch the World through Prayer*.

Take Advantage of Furlough Opportunities

Personalized missionary support is also very necessary when the cross-cultural workers come home on furlough. This may come as a surprise to us. We picture furlough as a time of vacation, rest and relaxation. But furlough also has its drawbacks, as Jim and Sue Kaiser, Lutheran Bible Translators in Sierra Leone, West Africa, openly admit:

Furlough Time is Here!

— and —

Yippee! Yay!
Family! Friends!
Ice cream!
Mom's home cooking!
Pizza! Movies!
Shopping in a mall!
Cooler Temperatures!
Electricity!
Christian fellowship!

Hmmm!
What's it like at home now?
Will people recognize us?
Will we recognize them?
How much has changed?
Will we fit in?
Where will we live?
Will we be able to tell people
    what it's like in Sierra Leone?
Will they understand?
Will they care?

(Kaiser 1988, 1)

These lines reveal many of the pitfalls of furlough time. There is reverse culture shock, that is, the need to adjust back to one's own culture. After being away for years, this is no small feat. The missionary must obtain housing, a car, and other domestic needs. This can be a real headache. There is the stress of renewing relationships, tinged with bittersweet emotion because before long they will have to part again. Finally, there is the difficulty of wanting to communicate so much, yet not knowing if people really want to listen. It is little wonder that the Kaisers add, "We'd appreciate your prayers as we readjust to U.S. living" (Kaiser 1988, 1).

In addition to prayer, how can you aid furloughing missionaries? Assist them in the search for housing, transportation, and other needs. When they come to visit, do more than listen to their presentations. "The hardest part about being a missionary . . . is being invited to give an account of your mission activities and observations within the brief limits generally allotted to a sermon in the U.S.A." (Danker 1964, 3). Set aside time to chat with missionaries about their work, about their lives, about how they feel about their work, and about their relationship with you and your church. Such conversation will flow quite easily if you have been building a relationship through correspondence, study, and prayer, as was suggested previously. After you have talked, be sure to spend some moments in prayer together. Through shared petitions the Holy Spirit will bless the tie that binds you.

Encourage Visits to Mission Fields

Foreign missions. Overseas ministries. Such terms imply that world evangelization is something that only occurs in places so remote that we never can get personally involved. But this does not have to be. You and your mission committee can help people touch, taste, and feel cross-cultural ministry.

Provide contact with local mission work. Organize field trips to ethnic neighborhoods. Visit with Christians who are involved in reaching out with the Gospel to the people there. Tour the office of a mission society or social ministry agency that is located in your area, learning about their work and how you might participate. Attend a gathering of international students at a college or university in your community. The list goes on. Be inventive. The more that people see the opportunities right around them, the more they will understand God's will for their lives and their congregation.

On a grander scale, you could help promote and direct a mission tour. Anyone who can afford a trip to Hawaii can get to mission fields too. Perhaps there is a former missionary or an adventurous pastor in your area who would be willing to lead the tour. Some time should be spent in seeing the sights and wonders of the country, but the major emphasis should be on meeting the followers of Christ in that place. Correspondence with missionaries in the country(ies) you hope to visit will help pave the way for your group to see the church of Christ in action.

Is Christian globetrotting a waste of money? A couple who had the chance to visit a mission field was troubled by this question (Krause 1986, 23-24). Finally, they sought the advice of a missionary on furlough. "If we had the chance to visit a mission field or to give the travel money to the mission board, which should we do?"

The missionary didn't hesitate in answering. "Go! Once you have seen the Lord's work first hand, you will raise more money than you ever thought possible. If you have the opportunity, trust the Lord and go."

Another way to help Christians come into direct contact with God's world is by helping them take advantage of their business travel opportunities. On one occasion, a businessman found himself in Mexico City for a whole weekend with nowhere to go and nothing to do. Upon returning home, he complained about his experience to a friend and lamented, "I've never been so bored in my whole life!" The friend, who was a world Christian, gave him the name and address of a missionary in Mexico City. On the business man's next trip there he had a totally different weekend:

> The missionary picked him up late Friday might, entertained him in his home, and spent the weekend introducing him to various missions and churches in the city. The man was so thrilled with what he saw that when he made his next trip to Europe he wanted the names and addresses of missionaries in the cities he planned to visit. Now wherever he goes he makes it a point to contact the missionaries and through them get a glimpse of the Lord's work (Kane 1986, 168).

Perhaps your job only takes you to cities on this continent. There is important mission work happening in those cities too. Ask your pastor for names and addresses of people who can show you the Lord's work in Toronto, San Francisco, or Miami.

Travel opportunities also exist for those who serve in the armed forces.

Maybe you have grown up in a community where there is little ethnic variety. If you would like to know more about missions, join the Navy and see the world—see it as God sees it. Or perhaps in an overseas Army assignment you will learn to be all that you can be, for the kingdom of God.

Send Forth Harvesters from Your Church

As you and your committee share the joy of missions and lead people to become world Christians, God will bless your efforts. He will move people to respond to His call to serve Him where His light is dim. How can you promote this?

Pray for God's Power and Guidance

Jesus taught that prayer is a key to recruitment. "The harvest is plentiful but the workers are few. Ask the Lord of the harvest, therefore, to send out workers into his harvest field'' (Matt. 9:37–38). Pray for laborers to go out from your church to bring in the harvest. Start right now, even though you do not know whom the Lord will call. The Lord of the harvest will honor your request.

Help people to understand what God's call is. Many Christians assume that a call from God to do anything must be a spectacular experience. If the Lord does not page them in the middle of the night as He did Samuel, they assume that God does not want their services. However, God uses such means only on very rare occasions. "A burning realization of the need, and the ability to do something about it, is often the only call, and a sufficient call, to enter God's work" (Voehringer 1961, 120). The mission committee will delineate the world's need and the ways to live as a world Christian. Having been informed, each individual must determine where God is calling him or her to serve in His name.

Promote Short-term Opportunities

Encourage people to test God's call through short-term mission opportunities. There is a prevalent myth that being an overseas missionary requires a lifetime commitment. In previous centuries this had some validity, for it took a year or more to travel back and forth to one's mission field. Commuting was out of the question.

Today, however, you can reach almost any place on the globe in a day or two, and there is a multitude of short-term mission assignments. The Lutheran Church–Missouri Synod has two short-term programs. Servant Events allows teenagers to experience cross-cultural or cross-environmental ministry for a week or so in the summer. Volunteer Youth Ministers are adults who teach English in the Orient for two and a half years, employing their teacher-student relationships to share Christ. Every denominational mission board and independent mission society has its own variety of short-term assignments. Intercristo Christian Placement Service can give you a broad overview of current short-term opportunities. The church mission committee should investigate the options and share them with the parish.

What is to be gained from a short-term experience? The benefits are many.

> The short-termer has an opportunity to be of real and definite help. . . . Though often limited by language on a short term, there remains the exciting possibility that both his enthusiasm and Christian love may result in either himself or the missionary leading people on the field to Jesus Christ.
>
> If this were all, it would be more than enough, but there is much more. The short-termer will see missions deglamorized. He will eat food foreign to his taste. He will know the bite of loneliness. The utter frustration of the language barrier will grate on his nerves day and night. So much to give and no way to give it!
>
> He will know the humidity of an unbearable climate, or the aching cold

of a hostile one, and wonder how people could ever stand to live there! (McElveen 1977, 17–18).

This experience helps the short-termer decide if he should ever become a long-termer. Some will be assured that they have the cross-cultural missionary gift, and they can plan their future with this in mind. For others, God uses short-term ministry to reveal to them that a missionary career is not for them. Grateful for the opportunity to have made a small contribution, they can return home to serve the Lord stateside or provinceside, not feeling guilty that they should have become long-term missionaries. In either case, God's will for their lives is revealed (Rom. 12:1–2), and the short term experiment is a success.

Promote Tentmaker Ministries

Cross-cultural ministry is not restricted to pastors and other church professionals. The harvest field is open to a broad range of professions and skills. Lay missionaries can be divided into two categories: support workers and tentmakers.

Support workers are those who work for a mission organization to make the ministry holistic, or to help the whole operation run smoothly. They include doctors, nurses, counselors, agricultural consultants, writers, professors, business managers, mass media experts, computer experts, teachers of missionary children, literacy instructors, mechanics, pilots, and others.

Tentmakers are cross-cultural worker-priests. The name derives from the apostle Paul who often worked during the day as a tentmaker and then spent his free time evangelizing (Acts 18:1–4; 1 Thess. 2:9; and 2 Thess. 3:7–9). Dennis Denow cites some of the tentmaking opportunities available in Asia:

> Innovative mission methods must be used. Specialized short-term lay workers will be able to enter mission fields because they possess some expertise desired and requested by the host countries. These would probably include education and business consultants, as well as social welfare, relief and development workers. While in the country, these specialists will have many opportunities for personal interaction with local people. Those most interested in Christianity can be identified and followed up by local Christian churches.

The most encouraging thing about modern tentmaking is that it opens doors where traditional missionaries are unable to enter. There are dozens of countries, with a total population around two billion, where the entrance of foreign missionaries is either forbidden or their activities are greatly restricted. Included on this list of countries is the most populous nation in the world.

> Explosive is the only description for the growth in the number of Christian professionals working in China. In 1982, about 30 Christians served in professional jobs. Today some 500 Christian professionals serve under dozens of agencies. Formerly most of them worked as teachers of English, but now Christians work as consultants, urban planners, professors, researchers,

health professionals, and business people (*Pulse* Feb. 26, 1988, 1).

If you are intrigued by this kind of mission work, read *Today's Tentmakers* by J. Christy Wilson (Tyndale, 1984). The text includes examples as diverse as an army doctor, English teacher, engineer, embassy secretary, teacher of the blind, lawyer, oil engineer, cattle raiser, and mining engineer. Communists, Muslims, and Mormons utilize the tentmaking strategy. So should the children of light.

Over the years, the Holy Spirit will bless your efforts and those of the mission committee so that several members of your church will be serving as missionaries. Some will be busy in cross-cultural or cross-environmental work in North America. Others will be short-termers and tentmakers. And some will be serving overseas permanently with a mission board or society. You will have accomplished the ultimate in personalized missionary support when you have friends in the mission field. Identifying with God's global enterprise, you will have become a world congregation.

While you are multiplying the joy of missions in your parish, share your global vision with other congregations, so that they too may join in the adventure to which our Savior has called us. The Great Commission is for all who bear Christ's name. Therefore our goal is not just to add a thousand world Christians, nor merely to develop a hundred world congregations. Our goal should be that all of us who walk together become a world church.

Do Something Now

Previous chapters concluded with suggestions about how to gain a better understanding of your role in God's worldwide mission strategy. This final chapter, however, has been one long "Do Something Now" list. Of course, you cannot do all these things right this minute, but you and your committee can make some beginnings. As you strive to make world evangelization the central, unifying activity of your congregation, more and more children and adults will catch the vision of what God has called them to do. That is multiplying the joy of missions. As you make mission work personal, the Great Commission will be transformed from a fuzzy, abstract concept to a heartfelt, flesh and blood expression of the Christian life. That is multiplying the joy of missions.

This is no small task which the Lord has assigned to us. How do missionaries keep lifting high the cross? How do "commissionaries" keep plugging away at their one-person-sized job in the global mission enterprise? What fuels their zeal so that it is not extinguished to mere embers and ashes?

Part of the answer has been presented again and again in these pages. The joy of our salvation motivates us to care about those who are perishing without Christ.

> The foundation of true caring is that we have ourselves been cared for, loved, and forgiven in a way that we do not deserve. Those who have grasped the meaning of that experience are so filled with wonder at the grace and

mercy of God that has come to them that they cannot possibly go on with business as usual or want to hoard that grace for themselves and their own kind. Those who know that Jesus Christ came as a ransom for many will praise God to be part of that company and lift up their eyes to see where else God may be working in the world (Lull 1987, 6).

The joy of salvation is a compelling source of strength for the world Christian. In addition, the Bible speaks of yet another joy which can revitalize us when fears and weakness overwhelm us. Nehemiah describes it best: "The joy of the Lord is your strength" (Neh. 8:10). With these words, Nehemiah urges us to sound the depths of God's love. The Scriptures state repeatedly that God's grace and mercy toward the human race find expression emotionally in divine joy:

> For the Lord takes delight in his people; he crowns the humble with salvation (Ps. 149:4).

> As a bridegroom rejoices over his bride, so will your God rejoice over you (Is. 62:5).

> The Lord your God is with you, he is mighty to save. He will take great delight in you, he will quiet you with his love, he will rejoice over you with singing (Zeph. 3:17).

The Lord rejoices in the rescue of men and women from every tribe, tongue, people, and nation. It is truly good, right, and proper that He should be so ecstatic. After all, He is the one who has turned our mourning into dancing.

The goal of God's global plan is that He and His church become an everlasting, magnificent, mutual admiration society:

> Behold, I will create new heavens and a new earth. The former things will not be remembered, nor will they come to mind. But be glad and rejoice forever in what I will create, for I will create Jerusalem to be a delight and its people a joy. I will rejoice over Jerusalem and take delight in my people (Is. 65:17–19).

May the Lord's joy over you be your strength as you face the challenge of your one-person-sized role in world evangelization. You will surely need strength to persevere, because opposition will arise. Some members of your church will favor the country club model of the church over the rescue mission model. Many will be so distracted by the maintenance needs of their own little chapel that they will not be able to identify with the ministry needs of God's church around the globe. This is nothing new. Both Jesus (Luke 4:24–30) and Paul (Acts 21:27–22:22) met with resistance, even violent resistance, when they expressed their concern for lost Gentiles. So when opposition arises, don't give up!

His joy in us and our joy in Him are twin dynamos that will energize you and all world Christians until Christ returns in glory. At times you may quail before the work that still must be done. You may long to be liberated from your sense of burden for the lost. You may grow weary of struggling against Satan, false religions, and atheistic philosophies. At such times of difficulty, fix your eyes on Jesus, "who for the joy set before him endured the cross" (Heb. 12:2). And you will be steadfast.

With the joy of the Lord as your strength, you will boldly persevere with the good news:

> Joy to the world, the Lord is come!
> Let earth receive her King;
> Let ev'ry heart prepare him room
> And heav'n and nature sing.

Resource List

Books and Articles

Adeney, David H. 1985. *China: The Church's Long March*. Ventura, Calif.: Regal Books.

Adeney, Miriam. 1984. *God's Foreign Policy*. Grand Rapids: Eerdmans.

Aldrich, Joseph C. 1981. *Lifestyle Evangelism*. Portland: Multnomah Press.

Astalos, Ronald F. 1962. *From the Diary of an Ambassador for Christ in Japan*. n.p. September 30, 1–2.

_____ . 1968. *From the Diary of an Ambassador for Christ in Japan*. n.p. February 9, 1–2.

Bakke, Ray, and Jim Hart. 1987. *The Urban Christian*. Downers Grove, Ill.: InterVarsity Press.

Barrett, David B., ed. 1982. *World Christian Encyclopedia*. New York: Oxford University Press.

Barrett, David B. 1988. "Annual Statistical Table on Global Mission: 1988." *International Bulletin of Missionary Research* 12 (January): 16–17.

Beals, Art. 1985. *Beyond Hunger: A Biblical Mandate for Social Responsibility*. Portland, Oreg.: Multnomah Press.

Beck, Hubert, Robert Lange, and Edward Schmidt, eds. 1988. "World Christianity—Vision for the Future." *Inter-Connections*, June.

Beyerhaus, Peter. 1971. *Missions: Which Way?* Translated by Margaret Clarkson. Grand Rapids: Zondervan Publishing House.

Bickel, Philip M. 1984. *The Noble Task: Counsel for People Considering the Pastoral Ministry*. Painesville, Ohio: Zion Lutheran Church.

Board for Communication Services. [1986]. *Take a Giant Step: Be a World Christian*. St. Louis: The Lutheran Church—Missouri Synod.

_____ . [1987]. *Mission Education Handbook*. St. Louis: The Lutheran Church—Missouri Synod.

Bobe, Louis. 1952. *Hans Egede: Colonizer and Missionary of Greenland.* Copenhagen: Rosenkilde and Bagger.

Bockmuehl, Klaus. 1980. *The Challenge of Marxism: A Christian Response.* Downers Grove, Ill.: InterVarsity Press.

Borthwick, Paul. 1987. *A Mind for Missions.* Colorado Springs: NavPress.

————. 1988. *Youth and Missions.* Wheaton, Ill.: Victor Books.

Brewster, E. Thomas, and Elizabeth S. 1976. *Language Acquisition Made Practical.* Colorado Springs, Colorado: Lingua House.

Brones, Dana. [1973]. "A Gospel for All People." Unpublished autobiography.

Bryant, David. 1985. *In the Gap: What It Means to Be a World Christian.* Ventura, Calif.: Regal Books.

Bubeck, Mark. 1975. *The Adversary: The Christian Versus Demon Activity.* Chicago: Moody Press.

Bunkowske, Eugene W. 1985. "Was Luther a Missionary?" *Concordia Theological Quarterly* 49 (April-July): 161–79.

————. 1988a. "Booting up for Receptor-Oriented Gospel Communication." Lecture from the Fourth Annual Missions and Communication Congress, Sept. 28. Fort Wayne: Concordia Theological Seminary.

————. 1988b. "Communicating Christ to the Yala People." In *God's Communicators in Mission,* ed. Eugene W. Bunkowske and Richard French, 66–79. Fort Wayne: Great Commission Resource Library.

Bunkowske, Eugene W., and Richard French, eds. 1988. *God's Communicators in Mission.* Fort Wayne: Great Commission Resource Library.

Bunkowske, Eugene W., and Michael A. Nicol, eds. 1986a. *The Body of Christ in Mission.* Fort Wayne: Great Commission Resource Library.

————. 1986b. *God's Mission in Action.* Fort Wayne: Great Commission Resource Library.

Burgess, Andrew S., ed. 1954. *Lutheran World Missions: Foreign Missions of the Lutheran Church in America.* Minneapolis: Augsburg Publishing House.

Buth, Lenore. 1987. "Where Missions Are Everybody's Business." *Lutheran Witness,* November, 8–9.

Carlisle, Thomas. 1968. *You! Jonah!* Grand Rapids: William B. Eerdmans.

Catton, Bruce. 1961. *This Hallowed Ground: The Story of the Union Side of the Civil War.* New York: Pocket Books.

Danker, William J. 1964. *Two Worlds or None*. St. Louis: Concordia Publishing House.

Dickinson, Richard C. 1977. *Roses and Thorns: The Centennial Edition of Black Lutheran Mission and Ministry in The Lutheran Church—Missouri Synod*. St. Louis: Concordia Publishing House.

Dorn, O. A., ed. 1962. *89 Modern Mission Stories*. St. Louis: Concordia Publishing House.

Douglas, J. D., ed. 1975. *Let the Earth Hear His Voice*. Minneapolis: World Wide Publications.

Duewel, Wesley L. 1985. *Touch the World through Prayer*. Grand Rapids: Zondervan Publishing House.

Elliot, Elisabeth. 1975. *These Strange Ashes*. New York: Harper and Row.

Engstrom, Doris. 1986. "Their Offering Shows Real Joy in Worship." *Personalized Missionary Support*, Winter, 2.

Dorothy Eschenbrenner. 1987. "Fingerprints—A Marvel of Creation." *Teachers Interaction Newsletter* 28 (November): 2.

Faasch, Larry. 1988. "Canada—Unreached Peoples." *Prayer and Missions in Circuit 8*, January, 3.

Fenton, Horace L. 1973. *Myths about Missions*. Downers Grove, Ill.: InterVarsity Press.

Gary, Olgy. 1982. *The Luna Game*. P.O. Box 5199, Chatsworth, Calif.: World Christian Magazine.

Gerberding, Kieth A. 1977. *How to Respond to Transcendental Meditation*. St. Louis: Concordia Publishing House.

Gockel, Herman W. 1968. *Give Your Life a Lift: Devotions in the Form of Modern Parables*. St. Louis: Concordia Publishing House.

Going, Barbara. 1986. "American Indian Student Aid—LCMS." *Arrow*, October, 7.

Goldsmith, Michael. 1976. *Don't Just Stand There: A First Book on Missions*. Downers Grove, Ill.: InterVarsity Press.

Green, Michael. 1970. *Evangelism in the Early Church*. Grand Rapids: William B. Eerdmans.

Hale, Thomas. 1986. *Don't Let the Goats Eat the Loquat Trees*. Grand Rapids: Zondervan Publishing House.

Halter, Carol Lee. 1988. *Newsletter*, Winter, 1–2.

Hanson, Allen D. 1986. *I Was in Prison: Personal Witnessing in Jails and*

Prisons. St. Louis: Board for Evangelism Services, The Lutheran Church—Missouri Synod.

Hanson, C. M. 1970. *Speak Tenderly to Jerusalem.* Minneapolis: Commission on Evangelism, The American Lutheran Church.

Heiney, Tim, and Beth Heiney. 1988. "Baptisms Cause Joy in Ghana." *Harvesters,* January, 5.

Hesselgrave, David J. 1978. *Communicating Christ Cross-culturally.* Grand Rapids: Zondervan Publishing House.

————. 1980. *Planting Churches Cross-culturally: A Guide for Home and Foreign Missions.* Grand Rapids: Baker Book House.

————. 1985. Lecture from Seminar "Cross-cultural Counseling," May 20–24. Deerfield, Ill.: Trinity Evangelical Divinity School.

Hieb, Glen. 1987. "Japan." In *Winning Souls,* Wisconsin Evangelical Lutheran Synod, 18–19, n.p.

"Hispanic Institute Growing." 1988. *FOCUS on Concordia Seminary/St. Louis,* Spring, 3.

Hoover, David W. 1977. *How to Respond to the Occult.* St. Louis: Concordia Publishing House.

Johnstone, Patrick. 1986. *Operation World: A Day-to-Day Guide to Praying for the World.* 4th ed. Waynesboro, Ga.: Send the Light Books.

Kaiser, James, and Susan Kaiser. 1988. *KKSL News,* May, 1.

Kane, J. Herbert. 1986. *Wanted: World Christians.* Grand Rapids: Baker Book House.

Kibira, Josiah. 1984. Opening Address. *In Budapest 1984: In Christ—Hope for the World.* editor Frances Maher, 13-22. Geneva: Lutheran World Federation.

Koeberle, Adolf. 1964. *The Quest for Holiness.* Trans. John C. Mattes. Minneapolis: Augsburg Publishing House.

Koehler, Helene Loewe. 1986. *Hold High the Cross: The History of the Lutheran Braille Workers, Inc.* n.p.

Koppelmann, Herman H. 1951. "Missouri Synod Undertakes Foreign Missions." *Concordia Theological Monthly* XXII (August): 552–66.

Korinth, Helmut, ed. 1980. *Dr. Martin Luther—Christlicher Wegweiser für jeden Tag.* Hamburg, Germany: Druck Offizin Paul Hartung.

Krause, Evangeline. 1986. *The Million-dollar Living Room.* Wheaton, Ill.: Tyndale House Publishers. Although out of print, copies can be obtained from Missionary Fellowship, Inc., P. O. Box 718, Austin, MN 55912.

Krueger, Ottomar. 1930. *Unto the Uttermost Part of the Earth.* Ed. L. Fuerbringer. Vol. 7, *Men and Missions.* St. Louis: Concordia Publishing House.

Kverndal, Roald. 1979. "I'd Give My Life!" *Mooring Lines,* September, 1.

————. 1986. *Seamen's Missions: Their Origin and Early Growth.* Pasadena, Calif.: William Carey Library.

Lankenau, F. J. 1928. *The World Is Our Field: A Missionary Survey.* St. Louis: Concordia Publishing House.

Laszlo, Marilyn. 1981. "Pioneering for Christ." In *Confessing Christ as Lord: The Urbana '81 Compendium,* ed. John W. Alexander, 205–15. Downers Grove, Ill.: InterVarsity Press.

Leupold, Ulrich S., ed. 1965. *Luther's Works—An American Edition.* Vol. 53. Philadelphia: Fortress Press.

Little, Paul. 1971. *Affirming the Will of God.* Downers Grove, Ill.: InterVarsity Press.

Lochhaas, Philip H. 1979. *How to Respond to the Eastern Religions.* St. Louis: Concordia Publishing House.

————. 1981. *How to Respond to Islam.* St. Louis: Concordia Publishing House.

Lull, Timothy. 1987. "The Key to Global Mission." *World Encounter,* Winter, 6-7.

Lutheran Council in the United States of America (LCUSA). n.d. *Social Ministry Affirmation: A Challenge to Lutherans Toward the Year 1990.* New York: Division of Mission and Ministry, LCUSA.

Lutheran World Federation, Department of Communication. 1988. *Together in God's Mission: An LWF Contribution to the Understanding of Mission.* Geneva: Lutheran World Federation.

Lutheran Worship. 1982. St. Louis: Concordia Publishing House.

McElveen, Floyd. 1977. "Why a Life Commitment?" In *I'd Love to Tell the World,* comp. Harold J. Westing, 9–19. Denver: Accent Books.

Miller, Peter. 1980. "Bali Celebrates a Festival of Faith." *National Geographic* 157 (March): 416–27.

Miller, William. n.d. *Tales of Persia.* Toronto: Fellowship of Faith for Muslims.

Missions Advanced Research and Communication Center (MARC). 1979. *You Can So Get There from Here.* Pasadena, Calif.: World Vision International.

"Mission Updates: Japan and Hong Kong." 1988. *Pulse* 23 (1 February): 1.

"Mission Updates: China." 1988. *Pulse* 23 (26 February): 1.

Mooneyham, Stan. 1985. *Is There Life before Death?* Ventura, Calif.: Regal Books.

Muck, Terry. 1988. "The Mosque Next Door." *Christianity Today,* 19 February, 15–20.

Mundfrom, Priscilla. 1985. "My Most Memorable Experience." *Lutheran Ambassador,* 17 December, 12–13.

Murphy, Alan, and Gene Murphey. 1987. "People in the City Need Jesus Christ." *Harvesters,* June, 4.

Murray, Andrew. 1979. Contemporized by Leona F. Choy. *Key to the Missionary Problem.* Fort Washington, Pa.: Christian Literature Crusade.

Neill, Stephen. 1964. *A History of Christian Missions.* Vol. 6, *The Pelican History of the Church.* Baltimore: Penguin Books.

———. 1970. *Call to Mission.* Philadelphia: Fortress Press.

Neve, Lloyd R. 1973. *Japan: God's Door to the Far East.* Minneapolis: Augsburg Publishing House.

Newell, William J., ed. 1983. *Reaching Canada's Unreached.* Monrovia, Calif.: Missions Advanced Research and Communication Center.

Nicholson, Dorothy. 1984. *Lord, It's Late but I Can't Sleep: Readings for a Christian on Mission.* Anderson, Ind.: Warner Press.

Nida, Eugene A. 1974. *Understanding Latin Americans.* Pasadena, Calif.: William Carey Library.

———. 1975. *Customs and Cultures.* Pasadena, Calif.: William Carey Library.

O'Brien, William R. 1984. "Commitment to the Future." In *An Urban World,* eds. Larry L. Rose and C. Kirk Hadaway, 207–14. Nashville: Broadman Press.

Panta ta Ethne. 1987. *World Mission Institute Bulletin,* November, 3.

Parshall, Phil. 1983. *Bridges to Islam.* Grand Rapids: Baker Book House.

———. 1985. *Beyond the Mosque.* Grand Rapids: Baker Book House.

Parvin, Earl. 1985. *Missions USA.* Chicago: Moody Press.

Patterson, George. 1977. "Facing a Different Culture." In *I'd Love to Tell the World,* comp. Harold J. Westing, 113–27. Denver: Accent Books.

Perkins, John. 1976. *Let Justice Roll Down.* Ventura, Calif.: Regal Books.

————. 1982. *With Justice for All.* Ventura, Calif.: Regal Books.

Petersen, Jim. 1985. *Evangelism for Our Generation.* Colorado Springs: NavPress.

Peterson, Robert. 1984. *Roaring Lion.* Robesonia, Pa.: OMF Books.

Pippert, Rebecca M. 1979. *Out of the Saltshaker and into the World.* Downers Grove, Ill.: InterVarsity Press.

Polack, W. G. 1930. *Into All the World: The Story of Lutheran Foreign Missions.* St. Louis: Concordia Publishing House.

Richardson, Don. 1974. *Peace Child.* Ventura, Calif.: Regal Books.

Roegner, Robert. 1986. "Fill Your Bag with Christ's Love." *Personalized Missionary Support,* Winter, 3.

Rudnick, Milton L. 1984. *Speaking the Gospel through the Ages.* St. Louis: Concordia Publishing House.

Scherer, James. 1987. *Gospel, Church, and Kingdom.* Minneapolis: Augsburg Publishing House.

Sease, Rosalyn, and Erich F. Voehringer. 1963. *Missions Today in the Lutheran Church in America.* Philadelphia: Fortress Press.

Selle, Robert. 1988. *Selle Newsletter,* January–March, 1.

Senske, Al H. 1988. "So You Think You've Heard It All Before?" *Sharing,* May–June, 1.

Shelley, Marjorie. 1977. "The Effective Twentieth Century Missionary." In *I'd Love to Tell the World,* comp. Harold J. Westing, 104–12. Denver: Accent Books.

Sidey, Ken. 1982. "Ordinary People with an Extraordinary Cause: Fixing, Giving, Going." *World Wide Challenge,* April, 18–19.

Sipes, Phil, and Mary Sipes. 1988. "Bimoba Get New Testament." *Harvesters,* January, 2.

Stafford, Tim. 1984. *The Friendship Gap: Reaching Out across Cultures.* Downers Grove, Ill.: InterVarsity Press.

Stokes, Richard, and Martha Stokes. 1987. "My Doubts Left Me: There Is Much Work to Be Done in Togo." *Harvesters,* June, 3.

Strom, Donna. 1987. "Cultural Practices—Barriers or Bridges." *Evangelical Missions Quarterly* 23 (July): 248–56.

Syrdal, Rolf A. 1967. *To the End of the Earth*. Minneapolis: Augsburg Publishing House.

Tappert, Theodore G., ed. 1959. *The Book of Concord*. Philadelphia: Fortress Press.

Tolkien, J. R. R. 1966. *The Tolkien Reader*. New York: Ballantine Books.

Trexler, Edgar R. 1977. *Mission in a New World*. Philadelphia: Fortress Press.

Trobisch, Ingrid. 1986. *On Our Way Rejoicing*. Wheaton, Ill.: Tyndale House Publishers.

Troutman, Charles. 1970. *Everything You Want to Know about the Mission Field but Are Afraid You Won't Learn until You Get There*. Downers Grove, Ill.: InterVarsity.

Tucker, Ruth A. 1983. *From Jerusalem to Irian Jaya: A Biographical History of Christian Missions*. Grand Rapids: Zondervan Publishing House, Academie Books.

Tyler, Jim, and Billie Tyler. 1986. "God's Power Is Strong in Nigeria." *Personalized Missionary Support*, December, 5.

"Urban Indian Ministry Begins in the Twin Cities." 1986. *Arrow*, June, 3.

"Urbanization—An Urgent Mission Frontier." 1988. *World Mission Institute Bulletin*, January, 1.

"Urban Outreach Strategies Being Developed." 1987. *World Mission Institute Bulletin*, February, 1.

Vicedom, G. F. 1961. *Church and People in New Guinea*. World Christian Books, No. 38, 2d series. London: United Society for Christian Literature.

Wagner, C. Peter. 1983. *On the Crest of the Wave*. Ventura, Calif.: Regal Books.

——— . 1986. "A Vision for Evangelizing the Real America." *International Bulletin of Missionary Research* 10 (April): 59–64.

Wagner, Stephen A. 1985. *Heart to Heart: Sharing Christ with a Friend*. Corunna, Ind.: Church Growth Center.

Warnke, Mabel. 1966. *Partners the World Around*. St. Louis: Concordia Publishing House.

Watkins, Morris. [1968]. *Christ for Every Tribe*. n.p.

_____ . 1987a. *The Great Commission Study Guide*. Fort Wayne: Great Commission Resource Library.

_____ . 1987b. *Missions Resource Handbook*. Fort Wayne: Great Commission Resource Library.

_____ . 1987c. *Seven Worlds to Win*. Fort Wayne: Great Commission Resource Library.

Weber, Leslie F. 1979. *Serving Others in Jesus' Name*. St. Louis: Concordia Publishing House.

Wilson, Sam, and Gordon Aeschliman. n.d. *The Hidden Half: Discovering the World of Unreached Peoples*. Monrovia, California: Missions Advanced Research and Communication Center.

Winter, Ralph D. 1978. *Penetrating the Last Frontiers*. Pasadena, Calif.: U. S. Center of World Mission.

_____ . 1981. "The Long Look: Eras of Missions History." In *Perspectives on the World Christian Movement: A Reader,* eds. Ralph D. Winter, and Steven C. Hawthorne, 167–77. Pasadena, Calif.: William Carey Library.

_____ . 1982. *The Kingdom Strikes Back!* Dimension Tapes. Bethany Fellowship, Inc.

Winter, Ralph D., and Steven C. Hawthorne. 1981. *Perspectives on the World Christian Movement*. Pasadena, Calif.: William Carey Library.

Yancey, Philip. 1988. "Holy Subversion." *Christianity Today,* 5 (February): 14–20.

Visual Resources

Bringing Christ to the Cities. 1985. Produced by Douglas Johnstone and Ken Peterson. 25 min. The Lutheran Church—Missouri Synod. Videocassette.

Johnstone, Patrick. 1984. *Overhead Transparency Series*. Bulstrode, Gerrards Cross, Bucks SL9 8SZ, England: WEC Extension Office.

Salifu's Harvest. 1987. Produced by Department of Communications. 15 min. The Lutheran Church-Missouri Synod. Videocassette.

The Story of Victor. 1985. Produced by Ken Peterson. 18 min. International Lutheran Laymen's League. Videocassette.

The Stranger in Our Midst. 1985. Produced by Campus Ministry Committee. 18 min. The Lutheran Church—Missouri Synod. Videocassette.

Wall Maps: Christian Aid, P.O. Box 1, London SW9 8BH, England. National Geographic Society, 1145 17th St., NW, Washington, DC 20036.

Audio Resources

Bakke, Raymond. 1987. *Challenge of Urbanization to Mission Thinking and Strategy.* Cassette. Concordia Seminary, Media Services Department, 801 De Mun Avenue, St. Louis, MO 63105.

Bakke, Raymond. 1987. *Strategies and Models for Urban Evangelization.* Cassette. Concordia Seminary, Media Services Department, 801 De Mun Avenue, St. Louis, MO 63105.

Francisco, Don. 1977. *Forgiven.* Nashville, Tennessee: Benson Company.

Green, Keith. 1978. *No Compromise.* Lindale, Texas: Last Days Ministries.

Westcott, Edward A. 1987. *Our Ministry: The Global Mission Challenge.* Cassette. Concordia Seminary, Media Services Department, 801 De Mun Avenue, St. Louis, MO 63105.

Lutheran Mission Organizations

All Nations Mission Education Materials, P.O. Box 5491, Fort Wayne, IN 46895.

Evangelical Lutheran Church in America, Division of Global Mission, 8765 Higgins Rd., Chicago, IL 60631.

Evangelical Lutheran Church in Canada, Division of World Mission, 1512 St. James St., Winnipeg, Manitoba, R3H 0L2.

Lutheran Association for Maritime Ministry, 2513 One Hundred Sixty-second Avenue NE, Bellevue/Seattle, WA 98008.

Lutheran Association of Missionaries and Pilots (LAMP), 9335 Forty-seventh St., Edmonton, Alberta T6B 2R7, or 3505N. One Hundred Twenty-fourth St., Brookfield, WI 53005–2498.

Lutheran Bible Translators, 303 N. Lake St., Box 2050, Aurora, IL 60507–2050 or Box 934, Station C, Kitchener, Ontario N2G 4E3.

Lutheran Braille Workers, Inc., P. O. Box 5000, Yucaipa, CA 92399.

Lutheran Church—Canada, Box #55, Sta. "A" Winnipeg, Man. R3K1Z9.

The Lutheran Church—Missouri Synod, Board for Mission Services, International Center, 1333 S. Kirkwood Rd., St. Louis, MO 63122–7295.

Lutheran Immigration and Refugee Service, 360 Park Ave. S., New York, NY 10010.

Lutheran World Relief, 360 Park Ave. S., 15th Floor, New York, NY 10010.

Wheat Ridge Foundation, 104 S. Michigan Ave., Suite 610, Chicago, IL 60603.

Wisconsin Evangelical Lutheran Synod, Board for World Missions, 2929 N. Mayfair Rd., Milwaukee, WI 53222.

World Mission Prayer League, 232 Clifton Ave., Minneapolis, MN 55403.

Other Mission Organizations

Association of Christian Ministries to Internationals, 233 Langdon, Madison, WI 53703.

Association of Church Missions Committees, P.O. Box ACMC, Wheaton, IL 60189, or 1620 S. Myrtle Ave., Monrovia, CA 91016.

Evangelical Missions Information Service, Box 794, Wheaton, IL 60187.

Global Church Growth Book Club, 1705 Sierra Bonita Ave., Pasadena, CA 91104.

Intercristo Christian Placement Service, P.O. Box 33487, Seattle, WA 98133.

Jews for Jesus, 60 Haight Street, San Francisco, CA 94102.

National Council of Churches of Christ in the U.S.A., Division of Overseas Ministries, 475 Riverside Dr., New York, NY 10027.

U.S. Center for World Mission, 1605 E. Elizabeth St., Pasadena, CA 91104.

Westminster Theological Seminary, P.O. Box 270090, Philadelphia, PA 19118.

World Vision International/Missions Advanced Research and Communication Center (MARC), 919 West Huntington Dr., Monrovia, CA 91016.